SHIFT YOUR THINKING: WIN WHERE YOU STAND

Entrepreneurial Thinking - 7 Strategies for Breaking the Code

Clifton L. Taulbert

Copyright © 2014 Clifton L. Taulbert
All rights reserved.

ISBN: 1500708356
ISBN 13: 9781500708351
Library of Congress Control Number: 2014913907
CreateSpace Independent Publishing Platform
North Charleston, South Carolina

SHIFT YOUR THINKING: WIN WHERE YOU STAND

Each player must accept the cards life deals him or her: but once they are in hand, he or she alone must decide how to play the cards in order to win the game.
—Voltaire

Dedication

This book is dedicated to all of those who are building their lives and careers in this dynamic marketplace of life, where ideas and dreams can become products and services. As you engage in this marketplace, remember that you have a choice in the decisions you make and the thinking you embrace to make those decisions. Always know that your choice of "mind-set" matters. This is your starting place. Don't allow challenging circumstances to imprison your thinking. You can shift your thinking. You can redirect your efforts.

    I remember the day the shift in my thinking began. I was just a young boy, a teenager on the Mississippi Delta, picking cotton along Highway 436 in Washington County. From my vantage point, I could see all the traffic coming and going from the city of Greenville into our small Glen Allan community. However, it was the rare sight of the Red Top Cab from Greenville that always caught my attention. They were rare sights indeed. I would stand and watch the cab until I could no longer see it—always imagining the life of those on the inside, either headed to or coming from the train station. I knew their world was different from mine.

    Cotton season, after cotton season I watched for the cabs, but I recall the day when something changed inside my head. Watching was no longer enough for me. Those internal conversations about others and their imagined success were no longer exciting. I was no longer satisfied with the culture of servitude brought on by legal segregation and the cotton world of the rural south. I wanted what I dreamed—a world beyond the Mississippi Delta, the heat, humidity and the cotton rows that seem to never end. That day, while standing on a cotton row that didn't belong to me, instead of imagining who was inside the cab, I pictured myself in the back. From that day forward, I embraced my new dream of myself. I realized that I could live beyond my circumstances. I didn't have to watch others. I could be a participant. Somehow I knew that one day my circumstances would change and that I would be part of the change. It was years before anything actually did change, but that hot summer day in Glen Allan, I shifted my thinking. I saw myself in the backseat of the Red Top Cab. I was already traveling beyond the fields of the delta. That day, I won where I was standing.

This is what I want for each of you: to know that you too can win right where you stand—in the boardroom, in your own business, in your work cubicle, on the loading dock, in your class teaching or learning, preparing for a sale or preparing to purchase, or wherever you may be at this very moment in life. From the day I stood up and looked beyond what surrounded me and pictured myself inside the cab, I started looking at my life differently and preparing myself for a future yet to materialize. I learned at that early age that I was the main character in my life's production.

This is how I view those we call entrepreneurial thinkers: as decision makers who follow through. In this book, I want you to experience the *inside of entrepreneurial thinking*—the *decision* and the *follow-through*. I want to introduce to you seven practical and transformative strategies that start with your "mind-set" choice. These strategies are not held captive by race, gender, geography, nor by the entrepreneurs we admire. These strategies are timeless and universal and will provide you the start and follow-through needed to find your place in your Red Top Cab. When embraced, these strategies are designed to maximize your potential, starting where you stand, and to bring about the creativity, agility, flexibility, tenacity and resolve needed to succeed wherever your personal, professional, and inventive journey takes you.

Contents

Preface
xiii
Chapter 1: Choose Your Mind-Set
1
Chapter 2: Be Determined
13
Chapter 3: Build a Solid Relationship Bridge
31
Chapter 4: Slow Down to Lead
51
Chapter 5: Know Your Business "Health" Metrics
64
Chapter 6: Be Prepared to Swim Upstream!
77
Chapter 7: Resolve to Succeed
91
In Conclusion
109
About the Author
117

Preface

It was quite interesting that night in Oklahoma City, in April 2005. As I listened to very successful entrepreneurs from around the country tell the stories of how their ideas and dreams became products and services for others. Although I did not consider myself as one of them, I heard my own story. As with mine, each of theirs included a cast of caring and supportive people who, just as in my life, had challenged them not to settle but to seize the moment, thus challenging their thinking and redirecting their actions. As each successful entrepreneur talked, I thought of my support team from back home on the Mississippi Delta: people who were field workers as I had been, but were always encouraging me to dream, work hard and study hard, all of which were essential to support my shift in thinking. Little did I know that my shift in thinking while picking cotton on Wildwood Plantation would one day thrust me into the world of entrepreneurs and provide me tools to experience various levels of success in all my professional endeavors.

According to former Supreme Court Justice Sandra Day O'Connor, "We don't accomplish anything alone." I know this wonderful quote to be true, and so do countless others, including those successful entrepreneurs from around the country being recognized in Oklahoma City by SMEI. I called my support team my "porch people": ordinary people, mostly cotton field workers, who, despite the system of legal segregation and the infamous Jim Crow laws, found reason and took the time to show their children a different pathway—one that would ultimately require a new way of thinking.

As my mind shifted from the world that sought to define me as inadequate, I found myself on the pathway that I had dreamed of and they had supported. The daily unselfish acts of my porch people built the emotional community I needed to nurture my dreams. Because of them (field workers themselves), I was able to think beyond the cotton fields that surrounded our lives. So can you, no matter how your fields might be defined. I was learning both the value of embracing wisdom from others and the value that was resident inside me. This combination of embracing wisdom from others and valuing myself would eventually change the course of my life. I didn't know it at the time, but I had embraced what I now know to be an entrepreneurial way of thinking. Not being afraid to dream and welcoming wisdom from others and having confidence in oneself is characteristic of those we celebrate and admire as entrepreneurs. Their way of thinking and responding to life is not a secret code. It is available to any of us, wherever we find ourselves in life. The entrepreneurial way of thinking is transformative. Embrace it!

My entrepreneurial way of thinking throughout most of my life was in part responsible for my being honored by SMEI in a 2005—one that was totally unexpected. It was all such a long way from the Wildwood cotton fields where I had first dreamed of life beyond what had been a way of life for my family for generations. I was honored by the SMEI (Sales and Marketing Executives International) Academy of Achievement, an organization dedicated to the celebration of the free enterprise system. By this time I had established my own company and was recognized internationally as a successful writer and for being part of the team that introduced StairMaster exercise system to the world. This honor placed me in the company of such luminaries

Shift Your Thinking: Win where you stand

as Mary Kay Ash, Edward Brenhan, Dale Carnegie, Steve Case, S. Truett Cathy, and Steven Covey. I had the privilege of being inducted along with John Sykes, chairman of Sykes Enterprises Inc., and Earl Graves Sr., the founder of *Black Enterprise*, a magazine dedicated to encouraging participation in the free enterprise system and entrepreneurial endeavors.

As I considered the past inductees and their successes, as well as those of the other guests sitting beside me that evening, I at first questioned my inclusion. Economically I was worlds apart from them. I was looking only at the end of their race, at their celebrated success and financial accomplishments, rather than at the timeless and universal process that had brought us all to the table. Somewhere along their journey, they had shifted their thinking. After considering my own journey I realized that I had displayed characteristics similar to theirs. I had shifted my thinking and refused to accept the status quo of the culture that had surrounded me as my indelible inheritance. I had realized I was not destined to work the fields of the delta, and that my story was still being written.

For all of us, our success was not just evidenced by accomplishments alone but in the fact that each of us, in our own respective ways, had embraced a winning mind-set. We had shifted our ways of thinking and started winning from where we dreamed. Such thinking had placed all of us on a pathway to success. I had indeed moved through life with some degree of success—from valuing education at all levels to becoming a valued employee, and finally to fulfilling a dream of being a business owner.

Without knowing the term or all that it entailed, I had embraced an *entrepreneurial* way of thinking during my teenage years. When I decided that I could be in the backseat of that Red Top Cab, something clicked inside my head. I was no longer daydreaming about the good fortune of others but of my own. I wanted something different for my life. I didn't know how it would all play out; I just knew that it would, and that my efforts would be in the mix. I had this sense that I could achieve what I dreamed despite the barriers I faced. As I said in the dedication, the day I shifted my thinking from the pervasive culture that had sought to define me, my actions began to follow my thinking. I won where I stood—on a cotton row that I didn't even own.

Sometimes we look desperately for that new place—somewhere other than where your challenges are, but winning at the old place—right where you are, can be your gift to the new place. There will always be a starting line, and it's usually right where you are. My thinking process has always been the force behind any success attributed to me, and it has also given me the will to persevere when life throws unexpected curves. Unexpected and unplanned curves tend to come in all of our lives, even those deemed remarkably successful. I know that these successful people we admire also have that "other" story.

However, this way of thinking I cherish today evolved over time from the wisdom of people I encountered early on in my life, who didn't have all the terminology, but possessed this sense of being able to recognize this valuable internal quality. They simply called it "gumption." They seemed to have understood that one could access a way of thinking and acting that would define your life differently. For my porch people, that winning, counter-culture way of thinking and acting was called "gumption." From them and from biographies of successful people, my way of thinking was being shaped. I have come to realize that in the world in which we live, if you refuse to give in to the temptation of settling for the status quo, this way of thinking can help you discover new and exciting pathways to a successful life.

Shift Your Thinking: Win where you stand

My entrepreneurial way of thinking has taken me far beyond the fields of the Mississippi Delta. I can readily see its' value worldwide. For some it seems rather new, but it isn't. This way of thinking clearly predates our modern times and was even present in ancient times. People were getting things done. They were continually proving that the seemingly impossible was possible. It helped to jump-start a new nation that we now call home: America. In fact, this winning way of thinking caught the attention of the French lawyer Alexis de Tocqueville in 1832 during a visit to America. He had come to study our Philadelphia penal system but discovered so much more. After returning to Paris, he captured all that he had observed in his two-volume book, *Democracy in America*. He very poignantly described what I would call a clearly entrepreneurial way of looking at life, saying, "The Americans always display a free, original, and inventive mind." He saw people winning where they stood, seemingly not afraid to shift their thinking and turn challenges into opportunities. Could this be part of our modern-day heritage—this way of thinking and winning despite the odds we face?

The porch people who mentored me were no different. They showed me the value of dreams even though many of them were not able to take advantage of the dreams that lived inside of them. Many of them saw their future through the lengthening steps of each child who passed along their way. Though hampered by the restraints of a system over which they had little or no control, they demonstrated a "push forward" way of thinking and sought to pass it along to me and to others. I believe that my decision to see myself in the back of the cab was in part due to the nuggets of conversation heard from them as they quietly spoke of the future they imagined while I was looking in their faces.

Clifton L. Taulbert

I embraced my porch people and everything they taught. They were my first mentors, instilling within me the notion that I could dream beyond the world that surrounded me. Their impact upon my thinking became reality when my high school graduation became a cherished accomplishment—but their impact would not stop there. It followed me into the military, where again I dreamed beyond what I saw. I continued to see myself in the backseat of that Red Top Cab, always dreaming of more than met the natural eye. My mentors' urging that I think differently about my future was equally apparent when I graduated from college with honors, and when I started my career in the health-care industry and then in banking in Tulsa, Oklahoma. All the while, I still held the dream of owning a business that I could call my own. For me the Red Top Cab was still in motion.

In the early 1980s, while employed in banking after five years in the health-care industry, I found myself in the once-in-a-lifetime position of facilitating the major sale of a small business. I was scared, but I also felt as if I could do this. I was watching others around me doing likewise—young professionals my age stepping out and taking risks. So why couldn't I? I refused to be held captive by my race! I could feel the urge of my "porch people" calling me to action. I could hear them saying, "All it takes is gumption." This was indeed my first time for such an endeavor—requiring building a network of advisors and becoming educated on putting "deals" together. I took a leap of faith and arranged for the buyer and seller to meet and for me to be financially rewarded.

At that point, I was convinced that I could make things happen despite the initial hint of apprehension I felt, and ultimately my earlier childhood decision to win where I stood on a cotton row that wasn't mine relieved me of those moments of apprehension. When the sale was completed and my commission check was in hand, I immediately took some of those funds and

Shift Your Thinking: Win where you stand

launched my marketing company with no idea of who my next client would be. I just knew that I wanted to own a business—a business I would call Freemount Marketing. Taking the leap to make my dream a legal entity provided me the fuel needed to take my dream to the next level. I wanted to honor Freemount Plantation, once owned in the late 1800s by my Mississippi great-great-grandparents.

It was the establishment of Freemount Marketing and Consulting Company that opened the door to several entrepreneurial endeavors, including being part of the team that introduced the StairMaster exercise system to the world. Being involved with StairMaster was a baptism in entrepreneurial thinking on so many levels. At this time, in a mocking way, the media was calling the product "Stairs to where?" Needless to say, however, the aerobic exercise world has been better served because of this piece of equipment and by the fact that despite the negative press, we refused to give up on its importance to health and wellness. Even after twenty-four months of no sales, I refused to give up. StairMaster is a household name today, and I still find it difficult to believe that I, this dreamer from the Mississippi Delta, was there in the early days. There was much more in the backseat of that Red Top Cab than I had imagined.

Entrepreneurial thinking would later benefit my passion for writing, which surfaced while I was in the military during the late 1960s. My first book, *Once Upon a Time When We Were Colored*, also became a success because I had learned to not give up. It was twenty years before those stories I'd started writing while a soldier were published. During that time, the rejection letters were plentiful. Most of my military friends found reason to discourage me. The war was on and maybe to them writing seemed too passive with the reality of Viet Nam facing us daily. I had so many reasons to quit and give up on my writing, but I refused to do so. I kept writing. I kept sending out query letters. And they kept rejecting my offer. I persevered. I had already won years earlier.

Upon publication in 1989, the book caught the attention of educators around the world. They valued the concepts of community that were included in the collection of stories. This further jump-started my consulting business through Freemount. Over time, *Once Upon a Time* became a national best seller and a major motion picture. I was applauded and celebrated, but few knew the journey I had taken before the book became reality.

I had learned to not give up. My thinking had changed. My response to life circumstances was not stopping me in my tracks. Had I given up when rejection slips came weekly, I would not have had the honor of knowing that Nelson Mandela kept my small book on his desk. I was told this by a member of the South African Parliament while she was visiting Tulsa, Oklahoma. I kept writing, and, years later, likewise persisted in pursuing my goals by convincing people that the StairMaster represented the future in aerobic exercise. This is what entrepreneurs do, and so can you. Entrepreneurs most often refuse to give up on their dreams. We celebrate their tenacity and fortitude, their way of approaching life, and yet I know such is available to each of us. I know you can win right where you stand. Your tomorrow's success starts today.

This way of thinking transformed my life and continues to do so today, and so I finally felt compelled to share what I had learned and experienced with others. As a consultant to industry, academia, and federal agencies through workshops, executive conversations, and keynote addresses, I am regularly provided the opportunity to bring together what I feel to be very significant strategies representative of the inside thinking of the entrepreneur. What we may have assumed to be a secret code accessible to only a few is continually being broken. The overwhelming response to my talks from diverse

Shift Your Thinking: Win where you stand

audiences validated for me that these strategies opening up entrepreneurial thinking needed a broader platform. Thus I decided to write this book and break the so-called code by sharing with others what has impacted my life and what I had learned from observing and reading about others who are described as entrepreneurs.

This "Shift Your Thinking" conversation started on that cotton row decades ago, but it really came to life for others with a speech I delivered in 2012 in Tulsa, Oklahoma, for Debra Ponder-Nelson, president of the Oklahoma Minority Supplier Diversity Council, the partnership of small businesses and large and well-established businesses in Oklahoma that focuses on diversifying the supply chain within the marketplace. With this speech she wanted to educate and motivate the audience to not settle for average. Over a few months, I distilled all that I had researched, along with stories of my own about not settling for average, into these seven strategies that I call the inside of entrepreneurial thinking.

The Oklahoma audience received these strategies with a standing ovation. More importantly, I was provided an opportunity to work closely with a major player in the aerospace industry. The regional manager of that company, who was present during the speech, saw the strategies as valuable assets to be leveraged by his management team in order to bolster their sense of ownership over workplace responsibilities. He recognized the importance of this type of thinking.

Later on that same year, in Denver, Colorado at the request of the president of the National Minority Supplier Diversity Council—Attorney Joset B. Wright-Lacy, I was invited to deliver a similar speech with the same focus to an international gathering of entrepreneurs, business owners, and corporate representatives from major corporations such as Walmart, Hilton Hotels, Wells Fargo, Starbucks, Booz Allen Hamilton, and

ConocoPhillips. Their response was the same as in Oklahoma. They embraced the seven strategies and demanded more; they wanted the "rest" of the story. The conference was filled with both those who had something to sell and those who were buyers. They were energized by stories of those who had persisted and won. They wanted to hear the Red Top Cab story one more time. They wanted to know about what I had learned from my great-uncle while riding in the cab of his 1947 International pick-up truck—one of my learning places. They also wanted to know more about one of my mentors, an older man we called the "Old African," the stutterer who despite his speech impediment sought to challenge us children to reach beyond what was at the time expected of us.

The Old African had stretched my imagination as well as the imaginations of my young cousins with books he had salvaged from throughout the larger community, and in doing so he had given us a much-needed glimpse of the world beyond our front door. He had the right type of thinking and thoughtfully sought to pass it along. The story of the stuttering Old African sharing stories with us after walking for miles loaded down with a satchel of books resonated with this audience of international businesswomen and businessmen. They cheered upon my closing remarks about how this old man, after reading to us would not leave until he had told us that we were marked for good. Though he never used the word "mentor," he was a mentor. His role in my life would be among those who gave me reason to believe that I could shift my thinking. When I saw thousands of people standing and waving the notes they had carefully taken, I knew it was time to step out and think beyond a one-time speech. The story of my mentors and their continuous impact was being applauded to become a book.

Both the speech in Tulsa and in Denver addressed the way of life and thinking that had made me aware that the future

Shift Your Thinking: Win where you stand

included me. Knowing I had a future was what I had needed as a young boy and what had held me steady during the time I was growing up around my porch people. I did not get in that particular Red Top Cab on the day my shift in thinking started. That was the day the change in thinking became obvious to me. I was a child. So I couldn't leave home even if the cab had stopped and beckoned for me. However, my dreams for something different and better became my new reality. Years would pass, but the day did come when I left home, and the Illinois Central became my Red Top Cab, taking with me the wisdom of my mentors and my own resolution to succeed.

For years after leaving my familiar surroundings, my entrepreneurial way of thinking opened the door to the possibilities that could exist. I had learned to think beyond what had surrounded me and had sought to hold me captive—at that time, the cotton fields of the Mississippi Delta and legal segregation. It would have been so easy to settle for the status quo that was grounded in a continuous history, as many of my friends did. I know they despised that way of life as much I did, but for some reason, they didn't see themselves in the Red Top Cab.

Change is possible. As a young boy, I was taught to make lamps from weatherworn tree stumps that had to be dug up from around the banks of Lake Washington. Just looking at the stumps, no beauty could be seen. Our imagination and our thinking would be necessary to turn those stumps into works of art. I couldn't readily see it, but our school's industrial art teacher knew what was hidden beneath that roughness. His voice to persevere pushed us forward. I would have to put in a lot of effort, but at the end of the day, those old stumps would glisten with multiple coats of stain. It amazed me that something beautiful and useful could be carved out of a stump that seemed to have no value at all. Embedded within entrepreneurial thinking is the notion of stretching the imagination and to become innovative. This is more important today than ever before.

My industrial arts teacher, Mr. Carter was one of my influencers. Our circumstances didn't matter to him. He had our future on his mind. I will never forget his energy as he pushed us toward success beyond the fields so many of us had known all our lives. Getting our hands dirty as we changed old tree stumps into works of art was his way of showing us what was possible with our own hands. Along your way, you will have your influencers as well. The key is to embrace such people when they show up in your life. Do as I did. Grab the old stump and take the influencer's word that you can turn it into art. You will have yours—those who will help shape your "push forward": that focused family member or good friend who keeps telling you that you can finish high school and college, the golf partner who insists you should start a side business, a college classmate who reminds you of your college dream, an instructor who pulls you aside and makes you aware of strengths you might have overlooked, the business associate who keeps telling you how smart you are, your selected Facebook friends and LinkedIn connections who value being connected to you, and, more importantly, that voice inside your head that keeps you continuously looking up the road for your turn.

Those defined as successful in their fields of endeavor are those who recognize that the key to success is to anticipate the presence of influencers and their conversations in their lives. When you have identified your influencers—people you want in your life, don't be afraid to reach out. Contrary to popular belief, most successful people welcome the opportunity to bring others along. They are ready to talk. You should be prepared to listen. Just as when I was a young boy, I am still listening today—listening for the guidance that moves me forward. Active listening is inherent in the thinking of the entrepreneur.

Shift Your Thinking: Win where you stand

They eagerly grab the good advice of others, add to it their own thinking, and run with it.

This way of thinking is of value in every aspect of our lives. Entrepreneurs are not averse to emulating the success seen in others—sitting at their feet, as it were, and soaking up the experiences they have to share, or even taking notes and perhaps sharing those notes with supportive friends. They are not afraid to think and act differently, to go against the grain, or to put in the time required to make it happen. They refuse to be held captive by fear of the unknown. They have no problem going where no woman or man has gone before. They intentionally embrace their sources of inspiration and release them for all to see, which itself is a form of winning. This is how the entrepreneur interacts with the world, and so can you. They don't have a patent on this type of positive response. Grab it! It will work at every stage of your life.

Today, legal segregation and its relationship to the agrarian South, which was my great stumbling block to taking chances on my dreams, does not stand in your way as it once did for me. But you will face many things that may seem as insurmountable and beyond your control—your own twenty-first-century roadblocks. These roadblocks might include financial issues, first-time innovators' jitters, marketplace constraints, fear of moving beyond the comfortable and familiar, and even fear of competitive forces. Don't park your life at these roadblocks. This is not the place of success. **You have to shift your mindset to embrace a winning way of thinking that values yourself and what you have to offer. This becomes your ace in moving forward from where you stand now.**

I want you to know that if such thinking can impact a thirteen-year-old boy in Glen Allan, Mississippi, and move his life beyond his twentieth-century barriers, this thinking will do the same for you and so much more. We all know such thinking exists, but often we see it as beyond our reach. We tend to think that these stories of success belong to someone we don't know and will never meet.

The fact is that such thinking does not belong only to successful men and women, such as Steve Jobs, Bill Gates, Oprah Winfrey, or Russell Simmons. We should ask ourselves these questions about such figures: What fueled the rise of their success? What was foundational to the creation of their companies? They were all driven by passion that evolved from having shifted their thinking to what I now collectively call entrepreneurial thinking. Yet that type of thinking is not exclusive to any one person or group of people. Whatever success may be attributed to me happened because I too followed my thinking and embraced my passion for success. I wanted my life to count for more than just surviving on the planet. I wanted to be successful so that I could make a difference in the world. I didn't always know what that success would look like. I just knew that it had to be different from the place where I stood at the moment. It would look like me on the inside of the cab.

From graduating from high school, which was a difficult task during that era of legal segregation and finally graduating from college to getting my first book published to being involved in the early introduction of the StairMaster, I always employed an entrepreneurial way of thinking. So can you. Be in control of your outlook. Be in control of your thinking. Win where you stand! This is how it happened for me. If you are to win and maximize your potential in today's competitive and rapidly changing global marketplaces, you will have to do this. To do less is to be left behind the curve, which places you, your life, or your company (whether you're the owner or an employee) at a competitive disadvantage.

The winning seeds of entrepreneurial thinking that were planted in my teenage years have produced fruit throughout my life. Such thinking will do for you what it did for me. It will take

Shift Your Thinking: Win where you stand

you to places and give you opportunities that you may not have even dared to dream of. As you read through this book, you will find me referencing my personal journey as well as validating stories of others. I have no doubt that it was that early shift in thinking that moved me from field hand to high school student to college graduate to business owner. I want no less for you. Imagine yourself in the backseat of your Red Top Cab, headed into your future—your dream.

I want you to maximize your presence in today's dynamic marketplace. I know you can. But I want *you* to know you can. In my business as a human capital development consultant at Freemount Corporation, my keynote speeches and workshops around entrepreneurial thinking are designed to change your perspective and help you to not be sidetracked by doubt or held captive by fear. It will help you develop new and meaningful ideas as well as redirect your actions when needed. Always remember, your actions follow your thinking.

Whether you're a high school or first-year college student, a business owner with years under your belt, an entrepreneur in start-up mode, a salesperson trying desperately to find your magic, or someone in the midst of your career run in whatever field of choice, these seven winning strategic lessons from the inside of the entrepreneurial thinker are for you. They are a ready reference to shape your thinking and your responses to whatever opportunities or challenges you are facing. They have manifested themselves over the course of my life and in the lives of countless others. Entrepreneurial thinking is not a secret code! These seven inside strategies are accessible to each of you. I know they will serve you well on your journey to success. At the end of each chapter, you will be called to reflection and action. Just remember, in today's marketplace, where change happens daily and quickly and opportunities are still waiting to be discovered, these strategies will become your reference guide to what is possible as you plan for your success.

The Seven Strategies
1. **Choose Your Mind-Set**
2. **Be Determined**
3. **Build a Solid Relationship Bridge**
4. **Slow Down to Lead**
5. **Know Your Business "Health" Metrics**
6. **Be Prepared to Swim Upstream: Easy is not Guaranteed**
7. **Resolve to Succeed**

When embraced and lived out, these strategies become the process that will help build, grow, and sustain your personal and professional efforts. With this entrepreneurial way of thinking to guide them, men and women once on the outside of business and commerce have been able to build communities of prominence—testaments to the power of these strategies when working together to sometime achieve beyond the imagination. This is how it has been for me. I am still on my Red Top Cab journey and continually being amazed as to where it is taking me. I want this for each of you.

These strategies will provide fuel for your innovative dreams, improve employee engagement, and promote personal growth at all levels. In some ways, this is our heritage as a nation—free, original, and inventive minds, as recognized by Alexis de Tocqueville almost two hundred years ago. This entrepreneurial way of thinking beckons all of us. Your next move matters!

Twenty years from now, you will be more disappointed by the things that you didn't do than by the ones you did do. So throw off the bowlines. Sail away from the safe harbor. Catch the trade winds in your sails. Explore. Dream. Discover.
—Mark Twain

Shift Your Thinking: Win where you stand

Personal Questions to Ponder

Before diving into the conversation, let's take a moment to reflect on where you feel you stand professionally and personally at this moment. Here are some personal questions to ponder before moving on.

1. Who are your porch people—your mentors? And who will be able to refer to you as their porch person?
2. How would you describe the culture that surrounds you? Does it promote stepping out and taking a risk?
3. What attributes best describe the entrepreneur you admire? Can these same attributes be of value in your life?
4. Have you had a Red Top Cab experience? If so, how has it changed your life?

Chapter 1

Choose Your Mind-Set

Choose your mind-set is the first strategy to start you on the journey of entrepreneurial thinking. This is the way of thinking I embrace today, but it came into my life as a teenager while growing up on the Mississippi Delta during the era of legal segregation. As a teenager, I shifted my thinking. I embraced an entirely new picture of who I was and who I could become and set out to live my life accordingly. It wasn't easy at first, but I never gave up and I refused to go back. I now know that I chose my *mind-set*. At the time, I was totally unfamiliar with the term or the concept of mind-sets. But thanks to the work of Dr. Carol Dweck of Stanford, now I understand that I had a choice regarding my future. My destiny was not set in stone: my choice of mind-set could make all the difference in my life, both personally and professionally. Your mind-set matters! I will talk more about Dr. Dweck's work on mind-sets later in this chapter.

The day I saw myself sitting in the backseat of the Red Top Cab was what set me on the course I travel today. It was indeed a starting place. I was unable to leave home at the time, but I knew that travel was in my future. Once the mental shifting started, I didn't need anyone to tell me it was the right choice; the actions I took over the course of my maturing years spoke for themselves. My physical circumstances had not changed, but a new picture was in my head. Those around me saw that I was not held captive by the fields that had been our way of life for generations. I was in the fields, but the culture of the fields no longer held my mind captive. I held a different conversation—one that was future focused and very different from the majority of the talk that surrounded me and our lives. Even though I couldn't articulate all that I dreamed and felt, I knew that a difference in thinking had occurred. For me, maybe I could call it the energy of expectation. I knew I was going somewhere. I was unsure of exactly where, but I knew it was a place unlike where I stood that morning. I was anticipating something new because of the internal decision I had made while standing on that row of cotton in a field owned by someone else.

This shift in my thinking was also recognized by others in my small community. I recall words from my Aunt Willie Mae—an entrepreneur in the truest sense of the word, but not described as such by those who knew and admired her. Being called an entrepreneur had not yet reached our neighborhood, but the concept had. Aunt Willie Mae was described by other adults within our small Glen Allan community simply as one who possessed "gumption." I have never forgotten the positive vibe of that word being assigned. Gumption could be seen and felt. It was a real personality trait that could set you apart from others. In small, but real ways, my Aunt Willie Mae had carved a pathway toward personal growth and accomplishments despite the legacy of field work that surrounded her. She worked in the fields as we all did. But she also sold pies and cakes to others and hired herself out as a pastry cook. I had watched her store away her extra cash. When accommodations weren't forthcoming for traveling African-Americans, she rented out her well-appointed front room to those needing a place to stay overnight. I witnessed her turn challenges

Shift Your Thinking: Win where you stand

into opportunities. While others may have been short on cash, she always seemed to have had the extra money that was so rare in our community. She was the bank to so many. I was a youngster, but her having ready cash did not go unnoticed by me. Her actions set her apart. Gumption was their word for her, but looking back at her life, she was definitely displaying an entrepreneurial way of thinking. She displayed a growth mind-set. To hear her say, "Lawd, Cliff is finally showing some gumption." was indeed the official stamp of approval of having made a shift in thinking. **Shift your thinking. Win where you stand.** It is indeed a strategy to embrace and implement. And such a shift will be recognized by others, just as Aunt Willie Mae's neighbors recognized her possession of gumption, and as she recognized mine. Making a mind-set choice was so important. It remains so today.

I wish for you to understand and embrace the importance of choosing your mind-set, this first strategy that takes you inside entrepreneurial thinking. A mind-set is the established set of attitudes and assumptions held by someone. It can be changed. You are never too old, nor too young. In fact, successful entrepreneurs of all ages are those who shifted their thinking, i.e., changed their mind-set, and then *followed through* on that shift. Choosing your mind-set is the starting line, but following through will get you to the finish line—to the sale you wanted, to the idea becoming reality, and even to the graduation you felt may have eluded you. Entrepreneurs tend to follow through. That's a time-proven strategy, not a secret. You can't win the race if you never start. Starting and following through is indeed the game changer. Only you can choose the way you want to start your day, live your life, and pursue your dreams, regardless of the circumstances surrounding you. Others may want the very best for you, but it is your choice and the actions that follow that will seal the deal. Your move matters! So did mine.

Your mind-set is a very powerful tool. Get to know and understand how to use it. When you make the right mind-set choice, you will more often than not follow up with actions and relationships that lead to winning, which will reinforce the decision you make. Consider your mind-set to be a muscle, one that becomes stronger with use and application. Not only will you recognize "muscles" growing as you exercise and apply your thinking, but so will others. An engaged mind-set is necessary to the achievement of goals. Maybe that is why in 2005, I was sitting with luminaries at the 2005 SMEI Awards.

According to British philosophical writer James Allen, "You are today where your thoughts have brought you; you will be tomorrow where your thoughts take you." The ride in the Red Top Cab was at first simply a thought in my head—a shift from wondering who was in the backseat to seeing myself as a passenger. However, it was that one thought that led to the change in thinking that continuously impacted my life's journey.

Knowing that you have a choice will be an invaluable tool for your professional and personal tool bag and foundational to your embrace of an entrepreneurial way of thinking. Embracing this mandate to choose seems to be inherent in those we call entrepreneurs. Early on I stumbled upon this fact that I had a choice, and as I embraced this new way of thinking, I refused to look back. This was one of the more valuable lessons I brought from the fields of the Mississippi Delta.

Steve Jobs once said, "The only way to do great work is to love what you do. If you haven't found it yet, keep looking. Don't settle."

"Don't settle" stands out to me in this quote and further validated why we admire those we call entrepreneurs: they usually refuse to settle even though settling is the easy thing to do. The choice is distinctly theirs. They are driven by their mind-set, not the negative conversation of others. We often stand back and admire these

Shift Your Thinking: Win where you stand

entrepreneurs' successes without knowing of the challenges they faced while making their victories seem somehow magical. Just admiring the victories without knowing the background could cause you to assume that the ability to choose one's mind-set is given out sparingly, and that it perhaps skipped your house. Good news—this is not the case. It showed up in the Mississippi Delta in the late 1950s and is showing up all over the world today. The opportunity to choose your mind-set is knocking at your door.

Choosing a winning mind-set is not out of your reach, and neither are the places it can take you. I know this for a fact. Knowing I was going somewhere beyond the fields ensured that I graduated from high school, where I performed what was required of me and oftentimes much more. It followed me into the military and was instrumental in my taking full advantage of the educational opportunities afforded me when continuous partying was a wide-open option. Years later, when my military obligations were fulfilled, that same perspective guided me when I accepted the opportunity for my company to lead up the government marketing for Stairmaster. Though years had passed, shifting my thinking while standing in a field in the Delta gave me the courage I needed to take on this challenging opportunity.

I had my starting line right where I stood, and I took off in my thinking without ever looking back. It has not always been easy, nor have projects always worked out, but I have always continued my forward push. This is what I want for each of you. This choice of mind-set is foundational to entrepreneurial thinking—a way of thinking I believe to be absolutely critical if you are to keep pace in today's twenty-first-century marketplace and beyond.

When lecturing or facilitating workshops, I tell my audiences that success or failure starts with our thinking, or with the conversation in our heads—one that we allow to push us forward or continually hold us back. You do have control over how you think and respond to the challenges and opportunities you may face. Your thinking comes from the mind-set you employ in your life and is the precursor to the actions that hopefully you will eventually take—actions that welcome the opportunity to stretch your imagination and be creative right where you are.

At no level of work or study can you do what you have always done and expect to get results that look like the future. If you are going to win in the twenty-first-century marketplace, you must be thinking about the look and feel of twenty-second-century demands—seeing yourself in your Red Top Cab. Dreaming beyond the cotton fields I had known all my life is what gave me my peek at the twenty-first century, but technology is advancing so fast today that we are already getting hints as to what the future might look like. You have to be ready to operate in a world unlike the one you know today. You will need the right mind-set if you are to be in the game.

According to the extraordinary work of Dr. Carol Dweck of Stanford University, as described in her book *Mind-set*, there are two possible mind-sets, "fixed" or "growth," both of which reflect the surrounding culture and have great influence on the personal decisions we make.

Let's start by focusing on the fixed mind-set and all it implies. From the work of Dr. Dweck, we can conclude that if people have a fixed mind-set, they believe that their talents and abilities are set in stone and that what you see is all you will get. They don't see themselves living beyond their current thinking and acting, and thus they ignore the potential for change that can be brought on by hard work and the pursuit of knowledge.

Even though the world that surrounded my youth seemed to have been set in stone, I dared to dream where I stood. I was

Shift Your Thinking: Win where you stand

ready for the hard work and the pursuit of knowledge required to be different. I wanted to move beyond the fixed mind-set that had trapped so many of the people who surrounded my life. The fixed mind-set is not supportive of entrepreneurial thinking. Those who subscribe to the fixed mind-set are not the Steve Jobs of the world, nor the people you have watched from a distance who have impressed you with courage, tenacity, and fortitude. Rather, those with the fixed mind-set tend to just settle for life and circumstances as they are, totally unaware of the potential inside of them to break free and become a new picture of themselves. **The fixed mind-set is all too common—showing up in our lives, our schools, and our workplaces and sapping imagination, limiting creativity, and often making us less proactive about our futures.** If you buy into this limited mentality, then the change needed to win becomes a real headache for you and an even greater one for your team, if you work with one. Limiting yourself can also limit them.

Your fixed mind-set is stuck at a place of non-productivity. The fences are up and reinforced daily. Your thinking remains the same, and your actions follow suit. This is not a winning mind-set. You don't have to do what you have always done just because you know what to do and how to do it. This perspective is more often than not the precursor to remaining average and can even lead to failure. To move forward and take advantage of what is needed to stay on top of your game requires a mind-set that has built-in flexibility and creativity and that is focused on the future. A fixed mind-set is just that—fixed.

Although it would have been easy to do, I didn't embrace the fixed mind-set, because of my porch people and their positive and continuous nudging. We all need such people in our lives. At the time, though, my early mentors had no idea they were inspiring in me what I would learn much later to be Dr. Carol Dweck's growth mind-set. I needed to hear my early mentors speak about a better place in life. Their talks were so important to my shift in thinking. Such conversations are still needed in the twenty-first century if we are to maximize our potential. The fixed mind-set will sabotage your future.

According to Dweck, "In a growth mind-set, people believe that their most basic abilities can be developed through dedication and hard work—brains and talent are just the starting point. This view creates a love of learning and a resilience that is essential for great accomplishment." Let's start our journey to success by embracing this winning mind-set. Dedication and hard work, key elements within the growth mind-set, are not held captive by successful entrepreneurs.

With the growth mind-set to guide my thinking and influence my actions as I embraced dedication to my vision and the hard work required to give it life, I discovered that I could be successful beyond high school. Overtime I realized that I could start a business—actually hire people to work for me and worry about payroll just like other business owners. It no longer mattered that "field work" was in my background and that legal segregation had welcomed me into the world. With this mind-set, over time I learned that I could create new realities. I surprised myself, and I liked those surprises. I learned that I could be part of the world's introduction to the StairMaster exercise system at a time when walking up stairs that were going nowhere was a media joke. I learned that I could write books and coproduce movies. I learned some forty years later that I could give a luncheon keynote address in Denver, Colorado, and give thousands of people reason to believe that the impossible is possible. Entrepreneurial thinking is indeed a game changer.

According to Dr. Dweck—and I concur completely—if you embrace the growth mind-set, you know that talents can be developed and that great abilities are built only over time. Embracing the growth mind-set is the path of opportunity

Shift Your Thinking: Win where you stand

and success, and it speaks volumes to the entrepreneurial way of thinking. Change and growth *are* possible, naysayers notwithstanding. You can win. Find your porch people—mentors committed to your success. They are not living on a distant planet that you will never visit. In fact, they may be right down the hall from you, sitting at the desk across from you, working out in your gym, riding on the city bus with you, jogging on the same path alongside you, just hired and assigned to you to show them around, or retired and looking for a place to deposit their wealth of knowledge. You need them. Look for them. They are still giving directions and holding progressive conversations.

This growth mind-set is needed in work and in life if you are to move yourself to the next level of success. On the other hand, the fixed mind-set blurs your vision: School and learning become a distraction rather than your opportunity. You can see the stagnation in your business. Nothing is moving as it should. The data is confirming that you are behind plan.

You seem to be trapped in this nonproductive reality. You know something has to be changed, but you fail to embrace your opportunity to be the change you are seeking. You have become comfortable with the familiar, even though it is obvious that the familiar is not working.

My porch people didn't know the concept of mind-set, but they understood that I had to hold a conversation different from the ones that were commonplace within the fields where we worked: "Boy, unstuck your head." I now know that they were telling me to shift my thinking to meet the demands of my future. Most often the status quo is not what we want for ourselves, yet many of us fail to challenge it. Why? We may not even like it, but it's familiar and it feels safe. Thus we continue to embrace it. You will not win if your nonworking routine becomes your guide to the future.

If you are not proactive in your thinking and well aware of your ability to choose your mind-set, you too can end up doing what you feel you have to do. You may be afraid to step out and explore what you want to do. This is not the way to win. An escape hatch exists. Think entrepreneurially. Business owners, students, entrepreneurs, and those of you on a solid career track, choose your mind-set. Just keep in mind that your mind-set can be changed. You don't have to do what you have always done, no matter how comfortable and convenient. If you want to win and "comfortable and convenient" is getting in the way, change your course. However, effecting such change starts with you. Your mind-set defines your perspective as well as your thinking and will determine the actions you take, which will be the signals you send. Today I challenge you to seize the moment—carpe diem.

When you embrace this growth mind-set, you will develop an entirely different way of thinking and of planning your day and the days of others who find themselves part of your team. It's a positive mind-set. It's inclusive. It embraces collaboration. Such a mind-set will keep you from being swallowed up by potential failure: loss of clients, the loan that didn't come through, or competition closing in on your territory. This growth mind-set will help you develop new and exciting pathways to your future and the futures of others. Tomorrow becomes an opportunity, not a burden.

I have adapted this timeless and universal growth mind-set to every aspect of my life. It is not held captive by successful entrepreneurs that we watch from a safe distance. Where it does show up, you will also see similar trends of success—people breaking out of the ordinary and casting fear aside as they marshal their unique gifts.

When talking to several of my business partners in the coffee business, I get goose bumps hearing their stories of the independent coffee growers in Rwanda, a country known worldwide for

Shift Your Thinking: Win where you stand

its suffering as a result of genocide. However, through the introduction of entrepreneurship, many Rwandans are smiling once again—growing their coffee, selling their beans, and building their lives. I have no doubt that their mind-set has changed from fixed to growth. This is the winning mind-set that makes the difference. In today's globally focused and highly competitive marketplace, this is the mind-set needed to foster growth and ensure success at any level of endeavor: starting out in business, growing your business, or in school and contemplating your future.

Choose your mind-set. This is indeed the starting place. It is so important to take control of your thinking. When your feet first hit the floor, decide to be a winner. Decide that you are going to knock it out of the ballpark or make the winning basket. You may hit a few foul balls or miss multiple layups, but don't quit. Decide that you are going to be the best manager possible. Decide that you are going to be the best boss on the planet or the employee whose actions take the company to the next level. Decide that what you have to sell can enhance the quality of life for those that cross your sales path. Decide that learning is an asset to embrace. This type of thinking sets in place the look and feel of the actions you take each day, which others will see and, if required, follow. *I can do this! I will do this!* Shift your thinking: win where you stand. The growth mind-set will travel with you throughout your life and will impact your response to the six remaining strategies.

Man can alter his life by altering his thinking.
—William James, nineteenth-century
American philosopher and psychologist

Personal Questions to Ponder

Let's take a moment and reflect on where you feel you stand professionally and personally at this very moment.

1. Have you ever given thought to the notion of a mind-set choice?
2. Have you noticed people who have a fixed mind-set? If so, what were the telltale signs?
3. What nonproductive strategies are you willing to lay aside in order to be a winner today?
4. How will you use the growth mind-set to take your business, career, and life to the next level?

Chapter 2

Be Determined

"**B**e determined" is simply a code phrase calling you to be strategically prepared—to position yourself to be firm in your decisions and ready to do the heavy lifting required to win. Entrepreneurs actualize this strategy all the time and win as a result of having done so. And so can you. Being determined is a key element in the entrepreneurial thinking process, regardless of your specific goals and objectives. Your adherence to the demands of this strategy will be driven by the mind-set you choose. The growth mind-set will push you forward, as it did for John H. Patterson, founder and CEO of the National Cash Register Co., who put sales training in place and with it a formalized approach to the effort required to win in the marketplace. Likewise, Mary Kay Ash has become a household name not just because of her line of beauty products, but due to being determined. Her approach to selling embodies being determine and has set in motion an income-generating process for thousands of women around the world. When one is determined, the positive impact can be felt far beyond the person and the place that set it in motion.

Many years ago, the African American community was energized with pride as John Johnson from Arkansas brought to life his dream of *Ebony*, a magazine celebrating black accomplishments. It began as an idea in his head. But like many entrepreneurs, he had to borrow the money from someone else. He had to find his angel investor. Once the investor showed up, he had to put in the hard work required—physical and emotional work. He was determined, and his determination created a new picture of our race throughout the world. To be determined is a must in the marketplace. We celebrate the entrepreneurs who push forward. Their success becomes the beacon for you to do likewise.

I am not asking you to become Karl Bushby. Do you know him? I want to tell you about him just so you can fully comprehend the universality of this strategy and how it shows up wherever the growth mind-set is employed to drive one's determination, for John Johnson in Chicago or an entrepreneurial thinker in Britain. At one time in my own young life, I thought that all the winning took place north of the Mason-Dixon Line and certainly not on a cotton row of Highway 436.

Well, Bushby is the twenty-nine-year-old British ex-paratrooper who is attempting to do what no one has ever done: walk around the globe on foot. To be determined is critical to his planning and to his expectations of himself. This persistence definitely requires a growth mind-set. Bushby's goal is not walking to the neighborhood park. We are talking about some twenty-five thousand miles—that's the circumference of the globe. Bushby wants the satisfaction of doing what no else has done before. This is not unlike many of you who choose to reach for the stars—to be positive standouts. He knows that completing the task to which he's committed will bring him that satisfaction. He also realizes that his decision to win is predicated upon him being prepared psychologically and physically. In this instance, Bushby can also draw from his emotional determination, which is essential to putting forth the effort necessary to ensure that he accomplishes his goal.

Shift Your Thinking: Win where you stand

This approach can also be summed up as "hard work." Being determined is the buttress needed to support your shift in thinking—to start your winning process. If you are determined, I guarantee that you can win where you stand. **Where you stand right now is your starting place.** Bushby is still walking and still determined to be the first person to walk around the globe. He has clearly embraced this entrepreneurial strategy. So can you.

There are certain qualities exemplified by those whom we describe as winners. As we talk about being determined, I am not asking you to become Kevin Durant of the NBA's Oklahoma City Thunder, known for his great determination on the basketball court. I am asking you to consider the process he undertakes to merit the athletic acclaim that he enjoys. That process is the reality available to each of you. Let's take a look at how Durant's process looks: It includes subjecting himself to the watchful eye of Dwight Daub, the director of athletic performance for the team. Day in and day out, he does the heavy lifting required to be the winner on the court. All the things we don't see or feel—the agony, the pain, and the frustration—help him to be prepared when it's time to perform. The behind-the-scene effort is what the fans do not see.

For both Bushby and Durant, being determined to accomplish their goals means being prepared on all fronts. They are driven by their internal commitment to be successful in their fields of endeavor. This way of thinking evolves from the growth mind-set—a mind-set that is available to each of you.

Once your decision to win is in place, being determined becomes necessary to take you onto the practice fields where the preparation takes place—the heavy lifting required to win the gold, to accomplish your plan. *The heavy lifting, the behind-the-scene effort, is not the glamorous aspect of winning in the marketplace. However, it is necessary. Entrepreneurs know this, and in their backstories are clear examples of the heavy lifting they had to do in order to win once the winning mindset was in place.*

According to Paul Graham, the noted English venture capitalist, "The most important quality in an entrepreneur [is] not intelligence but determination." To embrace this latter quality will serve you well on all fronts of life, being an entrepreneur notwithstanding.

In the delta, I learned early on from my influencers that I needed to dream and be prepared to work those dreams out. I needed to study hard when others were playing. I learned from my great-uncle as he brought me into his multiple small businesses while my friends were playing T-ball. Success depends upon our dedication to the work required. It was true while growing up and remains so today. To win in life and in the marketplace, sacrifices are required—like working out under the watchful eye of your performance coach. Working hard is not to be shunned as a potential plague. Hard work is part of the process that all must adhere to if they desire success—even the entrepreneurs we admire.

We all celebrate entrepreneurs. We celebrate their winning spirits. We buy their biographies. We celebrate their going public and the rapid rise of their initial stock offerings. It's exciting to do so. However, in those euphoric moments, we tend to overlook their laborious journeys to Wall Street and elsewhere—the going in early, pulling all-nighters, fun-filled plans for the weekend sabotaged by more work and more black coffee, and friends who refuse to understand why they continually reject invitations to hang out.

Sustained winning is about the hard work required regardless of your position within the company or where you are in life. It's about embracing a sense of ownership, which calls for a determined attitude that can positively impact any area of your life. Part of the payoff that entrepreneurs enjoy is their private

Shift Your Thinking: Win where you stand

knowledge of the effort they have expended to get it done. Yet their backstory of effort expended can be yours, no matter your profession or where you are at this moment on your journey. Whether banker or baker, your success will be determined by your commitment to the work required to set you apart from the norm. Good bread is not automatic; nor is a solid loan portfolio. Someone turned determination into action in both cases.

I recently read a story about a forty-five-year-old man named Hall Newbegin, who decided to take on Paris, France, and the fragrance business. This man wanted to introduce a certain wilderness fragrance—one that was at odds with the established marketplace. He was holding great conversations with all the right people but getting no traction. He was getting stop signs instead of go signs. Just as the successful banker or baker, he had to make a decision. He had to convert determination into action. This is what entrepreneurs do. They don't allow the fixed mind-set to determine the outcome of their dreams. With the growth mind-set to guide them instead, their entrepreneurial thinking kicks in, and they are off to the races. This thinking process can be yours too. What will you do if it looks as if you are too late to accomplish your dream? The average person will accept it, but not the entrepreneurial thinker. Even the media was telling this entrepreneur that Paris owned the fragrance market. Nevertheless, he decided to follow his dream and, over time, brought others along. But this conversation is not about the fragrance business. It is about the outcome of being determined. I want this to be your story.

Yes, Hall Newbegin has become very successful. However, his success did not occur overnight. He faced times when it looked as if the media were right and his hunch were wrong. Failure lurked around each bend, but his vision drove him farther into the wild. Newbegin's success has been a fifteen-year journey for him and his team, armed with pickup trucks and all sorts of climbing gear and cutting tools, to get the recognition he now enjoys. Once his decision became action oriented, he was on his way to success. The heavy lifting had him and his team trekking through the wilds of California in search of scents that were clearly outdoors—defying everything Paris was telling him. He knew what he wanted and would accept nothing less. To follow his passion took great tenacity on his part, and with all the walking through rugged wilderness terrain, it was hard on his feet as well. However, his thinking won out. So can yours.

Newbegin's Juniper Ridge products are now being sold online and at selected boutique retailers throughout the country, only because he was determined to make it happen and to do the heavy lifting required to win. Success is not easy, even if placing products on shelves is. But to get to that place requires a determined attitude. Newbegin's actions followed his thinking, and so should yours.

Being determined means being committed to the rigorous work your personal vision or the corporate vision will require of you. Newbegin was driven by his vision. Vision is important: it is that emotional picture of the practical journey you want to take. It's me standing up in Miss Jefferies's cotton field and deciding that one day I would be a passenger in the Red Top Cab. I would no longer be focusing on those "others." I wasn't sure of all that would be required, but I was determined to be a passenger, not just an observer.

This is about the team that will win because they have put in the practice time, worked out on their off time, and adhered to the health regimen required to have a physical presence and readily meet the challenges their opponents will bring to the game. In the marketplace, your competitive forces are gearing up to reduce your standing, to cut into your market share, and to slice your sales. To be determined is to be vigilant day in and

Shift Your Thinking: Win where you stand

day out. This is your competitive edge. At the end of the day, this is how winning will look.

Just as for Hall Newbegin and his wilderness fragrance company, California also provided me with an opportunity to stretch my imagination regarding what our company could do. I remember my first major contract that stretched my small company beyond Oklahoma. I was a subcontractor to the prime contractor for the state of California. When I first got the contract, I thought of the payoff and what this could mean for my company. I ran the numbers several times and more. However, in the midst of celebrating the potential, reality hit me, and it's good that it did. It dawned on me that I could lose that contract just as quickly as I had been awarded it. The fine print in the contract outlined all the requirements—the behind-the-scene effort I had to expend. We had been asked to design curricula for use in California prisons and to train the teams that would be implementing what we had designed.

The excitement over the potential return soon gave way to the reality of the actions that would be required of me. Instead of being daunted by the work required, however, I hit the practice field, as it were. I went into research mode to examine what had not worked in the past. I talked with prison management from other states to get their insights. My hour-long lunches became ten-minute snacks, and the weekends became part of the work week rolled into one long continuum. Sample passages were required, and so was the time needed to redo them, as I had to meet the "high" expectations of the prime contractor. But eventually the behind-the-scenes hard work paid off. Like Kevin Durant, I was in the game. **To be determined means that you are prepared to put forth the effort your success will require.**

This is also about creating new pathways, which will be easier for some than others—almost natural, it might seem. But that is not to say that your commitment to hard work can't get you there. You may not have what seems like a natural gift that someone else has, but you do have the ability to practice your way to the level of your potential. Dr. Dweck's research validates the idea that effort and hard work can keep you in the game and also make you the winner you deserve to be.

I had to learn to be prepared and do what was required not only for our California opportunity, but for an opportunity closer to home. Let me tell you a little bit more about StairMaster. This aerobic equipment company was born in Tulsa, Oklahoma, where I live. Tulsa did not have a reputation as a center for fitness innovation. We were known for oil and gas. Nevertheless, I had a hunch that this machine could actually accomplish what the inventor, Lanny Potts, said it would. It was a fledgling invention at best, but I followed my hunch and signed on to develop the entire government market for this company. I had no idea what would be required of me. I had the four-color brochures and knew the inventor. I thought that would be all I needed to knock it out of the ballpark. I was determined. I could feel it in my bones. I was excited.

However, I soon learned that excitement does not equal the hard work required. Excitement is a necessary precursor to success, but it is not the heavy lifting needed to win at the end of the day. Knowing this difference and responding accordingly is what will set you apart as a winner.

In those early years with StairMaster, I came to understand the deep meaning of being determined to win. I had multiple opportunities to give up. It would have been easy to do so. I had enough negative history hanging over me to justify such a decision. However, I chose not to give up and not to quit. Extraordinary men and women do this every day. Without this attitude, we would not have the greatest economy on the face of the earth—an economy that many describe as owing its existence to an entrepreneurial way of thinking.

Shift Your Thinking: Win where you stand

To accept the challenge of StairMaster and not cave in to defeat, I went into what I now call the "I am determined" mode. The four-color brochures were great, but they weren't selling a single unit. Something more was required of me. I had to bring head, heart, feet, and hands to the process. Well, after almost two years of diligence and hard work—researching, learning about the physiological impact of this type of exercise, traveling across the country, and being turned down most of the time—the preparation to win finally paid off.

During the interim before those sales started, I traveled a lot and endured a lot of disappointment. The product was new. It was not selling itself, and no major stories had been written about its benefits. But I was determined. This meant that I had to be willing to take my initial excitement and turn it into the daily grind of work. I practiced to be as good as the knowledgeable competition, and I embraced the hard work required to become part of a winning team, despite the embarrassing moments when I was not fully up to speed about aerobic exercise and its benefits. I had to learn all of this. It was like returning to school at night with no diploma at the end of my efforts—just the satisfaction of knowing what I was talking about.

While I was trying to make all of this work for me, I remembered one of my porch people, Mama Ponk. From my early youth on, she had instilled in me a desire to embrace excellence. To make sure that I understood that average was not acceptable, she had insisted that I read books. This was not something I wanted to do. Every other boy was outside playing ball, but not me. I would be sequestered in her front room with a pile of cast-off college books, where she would tell me, "If they can write it, you can read it."

Her vision was my education. Legal segregation said I could not avail myself of the public library. She built her own—multiple orange crates painted a horrible brown and stacked one on top of the other. She got it done, and I read books.

Those college books didn't look appealing to a young boy, and neither did the various university research studies on the heart and aerobic exercise that I needed to know in order to sell StairMaster. But once again I had to move that dial beyond average and acceptable to excellent and better. It paid off not only for me but for the health and physical fitness of people all over the country.

I had tapped into the persistent attitude of the porch people. I am so glad I paid attention to their visionary conversations and the winning insights they'd gathered along their journeys. Being persistent is what mentors do, then and now: their involvement in your life provides you with a wealth of information and examples to follow when needed. Unselfish mentors share generously from their personal and professional lives. Little did I know that while I thought I was just being a good kid and responding obediently, I in had fact been laying the foundation for a future way of looking at life, a way of thinking and responding that I would eventually utilize in all my endeavors. I learned from my mentors that there's nothing wrong in asking questions, finding answers, and growing your body of knowledge. Being embarrassed to ask is not the attitude of the entrepreneur, who instead tends to show up with a yellow pad in hand. You can do likewise as you welcome mentors into your life. Nothing is keeping you from acquiring mentors, rolling up your sleeves, and focusing your gaze on the horizon where your winning future awaits you.

One of my entrepreneurial heroes is Reginald Lewis, an African American who, unlike me, was born into a middle-class family in Baltimore, Maryland. Born in 1942, he came of age professionally when his dreams of inclusive corporate success had not yet been tested. Lewis died in 1993, but not before crossing a bridge that no African American businessman or businesswoman had crossed before. We never met, but I always

Shift Your Thinking: Win where you stand

admired him from a distance. However, his entrepreneurial way of thinking and the results thereof placed him on my mantle of corporate heroes.

Entrepreneurial heroes nearly always face the reality of being ahead of their time. They are powerful visionaries who are not afraid to dream. Who would have believed, for instance, that the small microchip would eventually revolutionize our world and give us Facebook? For Lanny Potts and his StairMaster, Mark Zuckerberg and Facebook, or Hall Newbegin and his wilderness fragrances, visions became reality. This concept was not lost on Reginald Lewis, who made a place for himself in the world and at the table of corporate America at a time when it was still unusual and unexpected of African Americans to succeed at that level. Today, many women and minorities still find the pathways to success difficult for a myriad of reasons—mostly historical roadblocks that have yet to be moved. Like so many others, I was mesmerized when I saw the magazine stories of Lewis's success, his attractive family, and his "toys." Now I realize that what I saw in those glossy magazines was simply the epilogue to a much greater entrepreneurial story, to life lessons for all of us and for all times.

What did Lewis do to get where he did? Let's take a look. Reginald Lewis was a consummate corporate deal maker who became extraordinarily wealthy in the process of his ascent. He was the young man who wasn't afraid to "think" winning, having adopted a mind-set that simply said, "I can do this. I will do this." His mind-set was not fixed. He saw what others enjoyed and saw no reason why he could not play the same game. He was not afraid to practice, to sacrifice, to get in the game, and to see himself as a winner while playing.

Wow—as a kid in the segregated South, I didn't even know that such a game existed, nor that as a black man, I was being left out. With legal segregation and limited access to participate in the business mainstream as my cultural backdrop, Reginald Lewis will forever remain a standout to me, and he should be to you as well. His reality becomes all of our possibilities: *If he can do it, so can I. If she can do it, so can I.* In reading about his life, it became obvious to me that he had captured the essence of success early on. Winning where he stood, he had realized that his own actions were his key controllable asset—his mind-set choice. That's right: never forget just how important your mind-set and your determination are to your success. Don't ever give up those keys.

Let's take a closer look at the corporate deal maker. For young Reginald Lewis, being prepared involved starting a paper route and getting up early to run that route. Eventually he obtained enough customers to sell his route at a profit to someone else. Even at an early age, before he bought and sold McCall Pattern Company for $65 million, making a ninety-to-one return on his investment, he had already embraced a different way of thinking and understood that being determined to win also meant being prepared to win. In August 1987, Lewis made history with the purchase of the international division of Beatrice Foods for $985 million.

Lewis's success was not without setbacks. This is common among most of the entrepreneurs we admire. And you will have your setbacks as well. His first attempt to take his company public failed. Yet instead of falling apart, he became energized. There was a back room of people who had set him on a course to win early on—his porch people, his parents, and the others mentors in his life. Reginald Lewis was not afraid to work hard. He understood the necessity of being prepared. He took the time and put forth the effort to learn the rules of the game. He was a graduate of Harvard Law School and courted those who were headed in his direction, regardless of race.

I certainly don't compare myself to Reginald Lewis in any way other than in the mind-set he embraced. It was the same

Shift Your Thinking: Win where you stand

way of thinking that allowed me to find a pathway beyond the fields of the Mississippi Delta and to follow my hunch with StairMaster. This is about the process that led to his success—a process that is available to each of us. Our destinations will in all likelihood be different from Lewis's, but I assure you that each of us can borrow from his example of determination to ignite our own.

I didn't become the golden boy with StairMaster, but I encountered success. My hunch was right. I learned that I had more capacity to win than I had ever dreamed of. On one level, I never should have tried to sell that machine. I was young and barely out of the United States Air Force. I should have known that the competition was too steep. At that time, the Nautilus brand ruled the fitness world, and their team of salesmen reflected that status. I was not in their league. The StairMaster was developed by oil field guys, not health nuts from Manhattan.

But like most entrepreneurs, I had this gut feeling that I was on to something. I heard Lanny Potts's story. I embraced his vision. That intuitive feeling was there, and it served to call me to action. It was in doing the action that I eventually realized my dream. This is the way it will be for you. You have to be willing to put in the time required to birth success. Know your craft. Know your prospects. Know your customers. Know yourself. Go the extra mile to be prepared to hold that winning conversation that sets you apart from others. Your sense of confidence will attract others. All of this, though, will require hard work and continued practice on your part.

Be determined to win not just in your conversations but in your preparation. This is where it really matters. Preparing to win was true with Reginald Lewis and also with Uncle Cleve, one of my Mississippi Delta porch people, for whom I worked as a budding teenager. He owned several small businesses that served our entire Glen Allan community, and I had the opportunity both to work for him and to be a beneficiary of his way of looking at life. He was a winner in the world during a time when winning was not easy for a black man. He was very firm in his decision to win, as exemplified by both his conversations and his actions. He was always forward thinking and never one to shun work. I introduced Uncle Cleve to the world in my first book, *Once Upon a Time When We Were Colored* which became a major motion picture. In the movie, his character was portrayed by the actor, Richard Roundtree. Roundtree's performance of Uncle Cleve as the firm and no nonsense businessman captured his entrepreneurial personality.

Reginald Lewis and Uncle Cleve were two different men from totally different worlds, but both adhered to timeless and universal principles that helped each of them win in their own way. Today I am learning from both. Their success principles are not held captive. Wherever you live *and* whoever you are, you must be determined to win. Once I realized that the cab that carried others could be my ride as well, I was determined to win, just as somewhere along the way, Reginald Lewis came to the decision that he could win where he stood. He shifted his thinking. He won in corporate America.

I am still determined to win. Of course I have moments, maybe days when I am overwhelmed, wondering if I made the right choice, but they don't last. During such times, I celebrate my success, no matter how small, and in doing so relieve my thinking of the negative conversations trying to find a comfortable seat in my head. I don't bemoan all the effort I put forth to be on a winning journey. It wasn't always easy to do the hard behind-the-scenes work. I didn't always want to do what was required of me. However, my vision spoke to my thinking, and I shifted. I took hold of what some may have thought was a secret code and decided to not let go. That was my choice, driven by what I now know to be a growth mind-set. To obtain the success

Shift Your Thinking: Win where you stand

you want for your life, the growth mind-set and hard work must combine to keep you on the right path.

I was determined while living in the delta. Once I accepted the fact that I could go and come in the Red Top Cab, preparing to win became the next strategic step to embrace. I doubled my efforts in high school and ended up graduating as number one in my class, even though my travel to high school was about one hundred miles round-trip on a daily basis. It would have been easy to quit school, but I had known from the start that more than a conversation would be required; I would also have to put work behind my decision. Those early days of not shunning the work required to get a job done would continue to serve me well. In the air force, I didn't look for the easy way out. I could have taken that route, but no—I used my spare time to take college courses rather than to keep the bars of Bangor, Maine, occupied with my presence. When I was discharged, instead of taking time off, I immediately enrolled in college. My Red Top Cab had changed, but the idea of wanting more had intensified. What I admired in others, I sought to bring into my life. And with that intensity, I knew that more would be demanded of me. I knew I wanted to be successful, and I was learning that success was being continually defined as my journey continued.

Now, keep in mind that this was in the early seventies, and equality in the workplace was not commonplace. After college, I ignored that reality and sought a position in banking. At the time that took courage—maybe akin to that of Reginald Lewis as he entered the world that attracted him. It wasn't easy goings. My pride was bruised. The fact of having been a soldier in a classified position didn't carry much weight. I was turned down a number of times, but I kept knocking on doors in Tulsa and seeking support from banking insiders at a time when all of them were white. I did become discouraged, but it finally paid off, and the hard work began.

I was in the game, but I wanted more than to be among the first African Americans accepted into the Bank of Oklahoma's bank management training program. The idea of wanting to own a business would not go away. While others talked of 401(k)s and retirement some thirty years later, once again I was holding my own conversation in my head. I dreamed of starting my own consulting business. Once you open the door to a growth mindset, you will be surprised where this shift in thinking will take you. Though the word "gumption" was no longer being used, it still resonated with me. Aunt Willie Mae was right. My shift in thinking was continuing to take me on a different pathway.

Being determined helps to set your course of action and how you handle opportunities and challenges. Behind the glamour of business ownership is the due diligence of hard work and preparing to stay in business. Hard work is the key to business and personal sustainability. I eventually became a business owner with all the printed stationery one would need, but I soon learned that much more was required. After shaking hands and passing out business cards, I had to jerk that tie off and do the real work of business: researching, making to-do lists, and fully understanding what my company offered. The dream is real, but it's only the door to the journey you will take.

What does determination look like? It looks like Kevin Durant, working out when no one is watching, sweating alone. It looks like Reginald Lewis, starting young and following through on his dream. It looks like Mama Ponk, creating her own library from used college books and orange crates. It looks like Karl Bushby, taking the first step needed to walk around the globe. Determination looks like Hall Newbegin trekking through wildernesses to find that special outdoor scent. And it

Shift Your Thinking: Win where you stand

can look like you fully understanding your commitment to your success and being willing to put in the hard work necessary to make it happen.

Determination looked good on paper for all of these individuals, but it was their hard work that got it done. Just remember that you are the key player in your dream. Shift your thinking: win where you stand. This is what I did and what countless others have done. The successful entrepreneurs that we all celebrate from afar all have their stories of how the journey really looked and how they played the hand dealt them.

> *I had to make my own living and my own opportunity! But I made it! Don't sit down and wait for the opportunities to come. Get up and make them!*
> —Madam C. J. Walker, African American, regarded as the first female self-made millionaire in America

Personal Questions to Ponder

Let's take a moment and reflect on where you feel you stand professionally and personally at this very moment.

1. Who would you describe as the most determined person you know? Can you list the qualities that cause you to define him or her as such?
2. How much time are you willing to give to see your dream come true—six months, fifteen years?
3. What does being prepared mean to you in your position today? Can you be identified as one who embraces the required heavy lifting?
4. Do you clearly understand that entrepreneurial thinking is not the exclusive domain of the prominent entrepreneurs we all know?

Chapter 3

Build a Solid Relationship Bridge

Now that you have embraced the growth mind-set and are determined to see your vision through, it's time to think relationships—those connections with people who will be essential to your sustained success, and you to theirs—people headed in the same direction as you. The marketplace, like life, is characterized by interdependence. People need each other. One is indeed a lonely number. The previously noted quote by former Supreme Court Justice, Sandra Day O'Connor deserves repeating, "No one accomplishes anything alone." The relationship bridge is a significant key to your success. No one understands this more than entrepreneurs. Building solid relationships is the key to their sustained success. This is clearly understood by those who make their living "buying and selling" in the marketplace. Building relationships for the moment, on the other hand, is just that—building for the moment. It's important to note that only genuine relationship building can ensure the long-term stability of the relationship bridge, which in turn provides for back-and-forth traveling and much-needed references. Entrepreneurs of all sorts clearly understand just how important people are to their success. This has been one of their supposed secrets, now yours.

Clifton L. Taulbert

Yes, people matter! This is true wherever you find yourself: in school, on the job, planning to start your own business, or running a Fortune 500 company. Peter Drucker, the noted leadership development strategists for corporate America, systematically called attention to the fact that people are the most valued element within the equation for marketplace success—and for success in your life as well, I will add. In the business world, Drucker realized the impact of the bottom line on decision making and planning. However, he knew instinctively that people were at the core of success. Because each person matters, it's very important to make internal and external relationship building at all levels a high priority.

This truth was not lost on those of us who grew up in the delta: people do matter. Without the positive impact of these unselfish people upon my life, I would not be at this good place today. People can inspire you to greater heights and also give rise to train of thinking that can change your life. This is what I experience as a young boy. Though our world in the delta was defined by the fields and legal segregation, I can recall with clarity how my mentors took the time to help me understand that people mattered and that relationships were like stepping stones to your future.

"Speak to everybody, and speak up," they would say. This is still good, solid advice, especially with the added phrase "speak up." My mentors somehow understood that your total being needed to be engaged in speaking; body language is part of the conversation. Of course, they didn't know the specific concepts of connecting the dots or body language, but as I recall in their very specific conversations, they were indeed helping me to understand just those things. I was building today what I would need tomorrow. I was preparing for my future by building the bridge I would need. My mentors knew that my success would depend on people and that the positive relationships I

Shift Your Thinking: Win where you stand

built intentionally would serve my journey well. That has not changed.

Relationship building is a key aspect of entrepreneurial success. Jim Clifton, the chairman and CEO of Gallup, said the following in a conversation in the *Gallup Business Journal*:

> Building and sustaining relationships is a key part of the entrepreneurs' success. Entrepreneurs must interact effectively with others. Successful entrepreneurs know themselves well and can perceive others accurately. Having strong talent in this domain enables entrepreneurs to connect and interact with employees, customers, suppliers, and investors in a way that results in positive business outcomes. Starting or growing a business involves interacting with many people. An entrepreneur may be the originator of the idea, but almost immediately, he or she must interact with others to secure resources, engage with potential customers and suppliers, or hire and manage employees.
>
> The enthusiasm and positivity of strong relationship builders make it easier for others to interact with them. These entrepreneurs also have high standards of personal conduct that enable others to trust them and form strong relationships with them.

Read this over several times and become very familiar with the actions required to build and sustain the relationships required for success. This is solid marketplace advice and applicable in all areas of your life.

The ability to build strong relationships is crucial for survival and growth. Successful entrepreneurs are adept at building relationships. They have strong social awareness and through technology can attract and maintain a constituency.

Though I'm impressed with advancing technology and all it can accomplish, I still highly recommend that you put in the face-to-face time necessary to build solid relationships along your journey. And it's still acceptable to send handwritten notes to those who have positively crossed your path as well as notes to those you'd like to know. In today's world of advanced technology, such notes are rare and much more memorable. They can make you the topic of a positive and memorable conversation. If you are to be successful, just remember that people matter. Because others thought I mattered early on in my life, I now find myself on this incredible journey—one beyond what I imagined while watching the coming and going of the Red Top Cab. Thinking others matters is where you start in this relationship-building process. Entrepreneurs seem to embrace this notion and constantly gather support teams around them. You can do likewise. Speaking to everybody is an easy task, but not one that everyone embraces. The porch people were right, and so is Jim Clifton in his analysis of entrepreneurs and their relationships. Building a solid relationship bridge driven by your choice of the growth mind-set can make a significant difference in your personal and professional journey.

Being successful in today's marketplace as an employee or business owner requires the embrace of an entrepreneurial way of thinking and clearly understanding the importance of building a solid relationship bridge. Globalization, immigration, and the impact of technology have created the need to be even more focused and committed to building a broad range of relationships. Possessing a growth mind-set is critical. Such a mind-set will place you in the position of not being fearful of reaching beyond comfortable—to reach across the ocean or down the hallway to get the job done. In today's marketplace, you will be faced with global opportunities at every turn. Just a few days ago, I had lunch with Max Scheder, a young recently graduated engineer. He hailed from California and New York,

Shift Your Thinking: Win where you stand

who now lives in Bartlesville, Oklahoma as an employee of at Schlumberger, an international engineering firm.

I had met this young man on the plane while flying back to Tulsa where I lived and where he was moving. Right off, I could tell that he displayed Aunt Willie Mae's idea of gumption. It was easily seen. I could hardly wait for our conversation to start. I could sense that he was an entrepreneurial thinker. He was focused. I could tell that. Just as I thought, a great conversation ensued and as I suspected, he was entrepreneurial in his thinking regarding his future. He had yet to experience his first day of work and was already thinking and planning next steps. I had no doubt that Max's company would benefit from the energy he displayed and the effort he would put forth. Entrepreneurial thinking was at work and building relationships was at the center. At his request, we exchanged contact information and agreed to stay in touch—another telltale sign of those with gumption. I am sure my Aunt Willie Mae would have spotted him right off. There we sat on a crowded plane, strangers at first, but no longer. It would have been so easy to lean into the window and watch the clouds or plug in the headpiece. Instead we talked. He was building his portfolio of relationships. He was thinking entrepreneurially.

Back to our lunch, weeks later...where I learned that Max, only twenty-two, was being sent to Singapore for three weeks. He wasn't afraid, excited in fact. I knew that he would make the most out of this assignment because of his lack of fear of reaching across the aisle to others who did not look like him or were culturally different. Sharing knowledge and gaining knowledge is indeed a hallmark of those defined as entrepreneurial thinkers. Building your relationship bridge is at the core of this effort. Max had already displayed that trait in my presence weeks earlier. Without embracing the notion that other people matter and having respect for the variety of ideas and customs he would face, it would be difficult for people like Max to work successfully on the international scale that is becoming more commonplace. This is just as important when working or studying down the street. Getting to know the people surrounding your life is an opportunity not to overlook.

To win in the twenty-first century workplaces, no matter your professional or personal goals, you must be able to connect with people from around the world and across the multi-generations of workers together for the first time in history. In the space of entrepreneurial thinkers, the various age groups are welcomed. Creativity does not regard age, nor gender or ethnicity. Most entrepreneurial thinkers value the dynamics at the intersection of experience and exuberance—getting the most of both worlds. Again, this is indicative of the growth mind-set, a way of thinking that is not afraid to build a community where the past, the present and the future can co-exist.

Part of that solid bridge-building process is learning the cultural languages and lifestyles specific to each of the generations that will most likely cross your path. In fact, linking across generational and cultural lines is essential if you are to maximize your efforts in the marketplace and in life. Solid relationships are good for business and for life, and they become the foundation for the business culture to remain competitive and committed. Embracing the various sources of knowledge is deeply ingrained within the entrepreneur's way of thinking. Entrepreneurs do not own this strategy! They just know how to exploit it, and so can you.

Building a solid relationship bridge is good for business. In your business, prioritizing relationship building is required from the CEO down to the last person on the loading dock. Building this bridge will require that all hands be on deck; it cannot be passed down the line for someone else to do. Entrepreneurs understand that each team member is a valued addition and

Shift Your Thinking: Win where you stand

establishing a good relationship with all members is the winning thing to do. This is necessary to ensure broad-scale commitment and accountability for the vision of the operation. This bridge building process can look like mentoring—embracing others, sharing knowledge and acquiring knowledge at the same time. In today's marketplaces, everyone brings value to the table. The vision becomes important. Your commitment to the vision will demand that you become committed to the people who will assist in giving life and legacy to the vision.

Just as I got to know young Max, and he got to know me, you too, are offered such opportunities. Most of my mentors were not related to me. However, we shared the same desire to be successful. Time and effort was required. Good relationships are valuable but not automatic. I had to nurture those relationships, and so will you. This is part of entrepreneurial thinking. Sharing and growing from the wisdom of others is not to be taken lightly. In unselfish mentoring, great lessons of life and business are learned and passed along. This was my experience while growing up in the Mississippi Delta and it remains just as valuable today.

It's also important to build and maintain a solid relationship with your external support team—your bankers, lawyers, accountants, insurance brokers—and others you deem to be critical to your successful outcome, as these people also play an important role in your success. Establishing solid relationships with these team members along the way is just smart. You don't want to wait until you are in the midst of a problem to call them. Find ways to carve out time to keep them in the loop of your planning. Early on in my career, I had failed to recognize just how important it is to have your legal and financial team in place and knowledgeable. My own personal background had not included such people; thus the value of mentoring. Don't be afraid to start off on your quest by asking questions and getting solid advice. Getting advice and listening have been a consistent lesson from entrepreneurs.

Growing up, my external relationships were mostly field workers. However, I had learned to value their affirming words. They weren't able to help me start a business or teach me how to sell Stairmaster equipment. However, their words of affirmation were critical to my shift in thinking to one day be on the inside of the cab and not just standing in Miss Jefferies' field watching it pass by. The bottom line is that no matter how brilliant your idea, or how brilliant you feel you are, you are not equipped to win this game of commerce or life alone. You will need the full array of mentors and advisors in your life. Taking a lesson from basketball, you could not win an Oklahoma Thunder basketball game with just Kevin Durant on the court. The team is needed, those on the court and those behind the scene. Relationships matter! A solid bridge upon which you can travel is absolutely necessary.

Entrepreneurs seem to understand this reality, and most are careful to nurture their relationships along the way, not just during the first day or week of introductions, or onboarding as it is called today. If you stop there, you have already sought to avoid some of the hard work that determination demands of you. Once you embrace the notion that other people matter, the next step is to nurture. This requires intentionality on your part. Figure caring about your contacts into your daily routine.

Let me introduce you to a lady who was also born in the Mississippi Delta, about a whole generation before me. I feel certain that her opportunities were few and that barriers to her success were plentiful. Even so, Willie Mae Robinson embraced a growth mind-set and shifted her thinking. In her world as in mine, the term entrepreneurial thinking was not a term in use. From what I have heard from others who knew her well, she was characterized by family and friends with having

Shift Your Thinking: Win where you stand

gumption—that ability to also reach beyond comfortable and build the much-needed relationship bridge. I am not sure if she had a Red Top Cab experience, but she did have her moment when a decision was made to take the train north. When she moved north to Springfield, Massachusetts, she took her entrepreneurial thinking along with her, her gumption as it were. She had already won where she stood, and packed her winnings to take along.

She's deceased now but is celebrated as one of the first African Americans to own a business on the main street in Mount Holyoke, Massachusetts, and to become a member of the Mount Holyoke Quota Club. She was an entrepreneur who valued relationships. I had the pleasure of sitting in her company as she shared the story of her phenomenal success. She had to build bridges between races, genders, economic differences, and ages. With the barriers of the Mississippi Delta as her cultural backdrop, it would have been understandable had she lost the will to follow her passion of becoming an independent business owner. Instead, her past energized her efforts and her obvious growth mind-set directed her actions. She met the challenges of Mount Holyoke and never looked back. Once her hair salon opened, she intentionally set out to cultivate relationships and build bridges. Not satisfied with success in the salon world, she tapped into real estate and won again. She knew that her business success would depend on other people, most of whom were different from her. Although, Mrs. Robinson grew up in the same Mississippi Delta as me—a full generation earlier, she had seen this growth mind-set lived out in her presence in small but meaningful ways. As I listened to stories from her sisters and brother, it was quite clear to me that their farmer father had set this way of thinking in motion, and no doubt referred to it as gumption. Relationship building mattered then and it still does.

Paying attention to relationship building has not changed; you have to build your relationship bridge. The twenty-first century demands this of all of us. Yes, it will take time, but it will be time well spent. Bridge building calls for being proactive, which is also a defining attribute of those we celebrate as entrepreneurs. You don't want to be known as the person or business owner who only calls out to others to stave off a pending crisis or to get you out of hot water. I know that the nurture factor is critical. I experienced it early on from my Mississippi Delta porch people. I knew it to be important. Miss Willie experienced it, as did Mary Kay Ash, and both ladies passed it along. The need for it has not changed.

Many very successful entrepreneurs actually factor in "downtime" to get to know their people. As a leader in any capacity, it's really good to know all your support people and for them to know you. Such inclusive relationships will serve you well during good times and bad times. We have to take the handshake to the next level. A morning nod is good but not sufficient to carry the day. A quick text has its place, but it will never be able to replace your face-to-face interaction. Never underestimate the power of your presence in the lives of others. We all love those calls and notes from friends and coworkers that start out by simply saying, "I was just thinking about you." Sometimes we call this "building community"—not a bad action to consider.

Building a solid relationship bridge is also about the importance of purposeful, consistent, and, most importantly, honest communication. In fact, honesty is a key component in the process. People tend not to guess the truth, and thus the need for honest talk. The truth may seem a bit harsh at times, but very seldom does it need to be explained due to unraveling—as would happen in the case of building a conversation with dishonest statements. Truth stands when you are not there to defend it.

Shift Your Thinking: Win where you stand

Mentoring is a key ingredient in building a solid relationship bridge. This term is bantered back and forth in our marketplaces. But what does it really mean? I have touched on it briefly in prior conversation. I want to take this very important topic a step further. Mentoring is so germane to entrepreneurial thinking. Most successful entrepreneurs as well as successful ordinary people have had mentors or porch people in their lives. Mentoring is unselfishly sharing time and knowledge so that someone else can maximize their skills, experiences, and perspectives. It is this up-close relationship building that allows for the continued growth of new ideas being brought to market and people becoming successful in whatever their field of choice. These type of mentors are able to see their success continued or dream realized through the success of others. The mentees' achievements become their rewards.

Do you know Ms. Duncan, a fourth grade teacher? Think real hard. She was unselfish and aided others in seeing their potential. She loved books and shared that love of reading with her students, even though her students may have been lacking in material wherewithal. She was quick to challenge her students to do more. The surroundings may have looked dismal and opportunities few, but her vision was beyond that reality. Ms. Duncan was thinking entrepreneurially. She was future-focused and the success of others mattered. Maybe you don't know Ms. Duncan, but Oprah Winfrey does. Ms. Duncan was her mentor. I can imagine that Ms. Duncan saw her own steps lengthening through those of her pupil. Both the mentor and the mentee seized the moment, but neither could predict the outcome of their mentoring encounter. Established in business, just starting a business, or in school, it's important to have that caring visionary cross your path. We will all need a Ms. Duncan on our journey.

I needed other people to invest in my life. Fortunately the porch people stepped up. They didn't have stocks or bonds to give me, but they gave me those encouraging conversations that were instrumental in shifting my thinking. We all need that caring ear. We all need that word of wisdom that comes from time and experience. Whether in business or in your personal life, when this "people-building process" is undertaken, the return on the investment of time and commitment will be recognized and appreciated.

I recall the dot-com era of the 1990s, when entrepreneurs were on every corner. Across the country and especially on the West Coast, they were known to be welcoming of new and exciting ideas and even went about building creative thinking places within their buildings to nurture relationships among their teams which they felt to be critical to downloading this pent-up innovative energy. Somehow, along the way, these entrepreneurs had come to the conclusion that they could get much more creativity and productivity out of their people if they created a climate that valued relationships and showed they cared. This is still true today. You need this. And if others are working with you, they need to experience "care" as well.

"Caring" is not a bad word. It is not a soft skill. It is the structural steel required to build the culture needed to give people a sense of security and a feeling of worth. Entrepreneurial thinkers are among those who value the contributions of others and are committed to maintaining their people and their contributions. If you are in a place where you feel you don't matter, your productivity or lack of productivity will reflect this reality. On the other hand, if you feel cared for, you are more likely to delve into your performance reserve for the benefit of the company. Entrepreneurs expect more. Entrepreneurs tend to do more for their people. There is no doubt in my mind that building

Shift Your Thinking: Win where you stand

the right culture—one where relationships matter—will aid in bringing about the success you envision.

I recall going into one major tech player's place of business in San Francisco (Ninth House, an international leadership consulting company), now part of Korn Ferry to meet with one of the top contract negotiators. When I arrived and was shown to his space, I also met his dog, who was sitting by his desk. I was a bit taken aback, but I am from Oklahoma, so I handled it. I patted the dog on the head and set out to negotiate a contract as a content professor. I remember the negotiator being so at ease, as was the dog. He was happy, and I smiled back, and the dog sat quietly—listening to the contract negotiations, I suppose. The negotiator was so at ease that my first-visit nervousness was set aside, and he ended up with a signed contract solidly in the favor of his company.

The story, though, is not about the dog or the communal space that defined the workplace, but about the ability of the entrepreneur owners of this company to recognize the importance of creating an internal environment where their people knew they mattered. Because they felt they mattered, they found it easy to keep the needs of the company top of mind. Jeff Snipes, one of the cofounders of Ninth House, wanted to ensure that nothing would stop the flow of productivity and creativity. Competition was still out there and their bottom line mattered, the dog on the leash by the desk notwithstanding.

Competition is the constant push in a robust business culture, and especially today, as globalization comes of age along with advances in technology. I don't think we are seeing as many dogs at work today as back then in the nineties, but the idea of fueling productive and creative relationships has definitely moved forward, with major companies now building in space that automatically brings people together. Bringing people out of intellectual isolation allows them to share their thoughts and ideas. Architects, for instance, are being challenged to design for collaboration.

I suggest that we take this noble plan one step farther. Be like the entrepreneurs and make your venture a story—one that you tell and live out and invite others to join. Set the example for what you wish to see and feel and lead in shaping the stories of your organization. Such a response starts personally and cascades into the workplace and the lives of others, becoming your strategic conversation in the marketplace of business and life.

As a kid, I also had my relationship-building space—not the same as the one I encountered in San Francisco, nor anything like today's Wi-Fi and other smart connections, but a wooden bench upon which my uncle and I sat and shared life. This was me and my entrepreneur uncle just valuing each other enough to share time. There was also Mr. Louis Fields, who lived down below the "colored" school. His home was always a welcoming place where he and his wife, Miss Sarah, would always have an extra place ready at their table, and I was always ready to occupy that chair. After our meal, however, we would sit on his front porch where the cotton fields came up close to his property line. While we talked, the fields were easy to see. Though in our own world, we were also invaded by the smell of DDT-a defoliant used to kill bugs. We ignored both, and I would listen as he talked about his life and my future. Thinking back to those conversations, they were so future-focused when it appeared that our lives would never change. His life had been lived, but he dreamed his future through the steps of the children who crossed his path. I was fortunate to have been one. I also know that talks and sharing of dreams with others will be required of me.

You too will need to plan to share time. You too will need your relationship-building space: a walk in the park, a game at Dodger Stadium, a beer together at the local pub, a few text messages that actually mean something, or a great conversation when together on a plane or in a cab on your way to an appointment. Even if you are a student, or just starting out in business, or working as an intern, take the time to build relationships. Don't be shy; be determined. Most of your peers will delight in sharing their lives with you. Take time off to talk. Building relationships is much more than simply shaking hands, nodding your head, and moving on. Take time to build trust. Take time to laugh. To laugh is to have listened. Take time to appreciate those around you by noticing their lives' incidents and sharing your observations, verbally or in a well-phrased note. This is part of the bridge-building process.

It is in the building of such a bridge that you position yourself for success in the marketplace and in life. Success is not automatic. You have to plan for it. The relationships you build and the nurturing of those relationships are part of the bridge-building process. I didn't just pick this wisdom up off the street while simply whistling along one day. I am a product of entrepreneurial-minded people—people with gumption. I took notice of their influence on my life and on the lives of others I knew.

In my young days on the Mississippi Delta, the field hands helped to shape my future. They recognized the limitations of their world but saw the future within mine. I took their admonitions to heart. I would need their lessons when I finally left the delta and Saint Louis became my new home. There my uncle Madison allowed me to not be overwhelmed by the requirements of the city. He and his wife, Aunt Dora, though not blood related, provided me a place at the supper table with his family and room and board at a rate I could afford.

Years later, in Tulsa, what I learned in the delta and experienced in Saint Louis would be of great benefit as I sought to enter the world of banking, which at the time had very few people of color in significant positions. Through my determination, Bill Welch, a Tulsa banker, eventually crossed my path and helped set me on my course in banking. My dream needed a bridge. Bill Welch became that bridge. From all these people I came to understand the immense value of building relationships. Their relationships with me changed my life, and I saw no reason not to emulate what had worked in their ways of thinking and responding to life.

Stepping out to help others may not always be easy, but it is always beneficial. It certainly wasn't all that easy for my porch people. Nor will it be easy in your world. Difficulty is difficult no matter when it shows up—whether in Silicon Valley, the Mississippi Delta, or on Wall Street. But despite difficulty, building a solid bridge of relationships is necessary if you are to be successful and remain that way. Treat everybody with the utmost respect—valuing their time, providing good service, honestly listening, and, most importantly, keeping your word.

It seems that most entrepreneurs understand the importance of this bridge and what one has to do to build and maintain it. From a very practical point of view, this relationship bridge becomes the road upon which your products, services, invoices, and remittances will travel. If there is a breakdown of this bridge—no communication, incomplete communication, hurt feelings, biases, products not up to par, or services poorly rendered—your business will suffer.

Conversely, if this bridge of relationships remains solid and strong because you are tending to the business of tending to people, your business will be a direct beneficiary of commerce going right. Secondly, you will have in your life people you trust and people who trust you. Engaging, inclusive, collaborative relationships matter, and they will drive the crucial elements of commerce that are essential to building, growing, and sustaining

Shift Your Thinking: Win where you stand

your business. To have a focus on relationships requires that most of us shift our thinking and be willing to start the process right where we are. There will never be a better time to build relationships than right now. This strategy reaches far beyond business and innovation, when embraced and deployed, it will impact our lives. Win where you stand!

This became very clear to me when I was trying to introduce the then-unknown StairMaster exercise system to the federal-government fitness world. I knew exactly what I wanted to do, but in my travels I had also discovered how much I didn't know. I needed people with knowledge to walk alongside me. I needed support and encouragement. I needed someone to walk into my life willing and able to help me make this business work. I needed a porch person—someone who cared and was willing to translate that care into sharing knowledge with me, a novice in the business. I found that someone in an older, experienced white military man. He reached out and I accepted his reach. Together, we tackled what I didn't know and what I needed to learn. Our budding relationship was the key.

Over the years, our relationship grew, and we experienced respect, affirmation, and inclusion (RAI). You will need all three today as part of your commitment to build your much-needed relationship bridge—a bridge that could possibly take you beyond your comfort zone, but where you need to be. You can ensure the presence of RAI—respect, affirmation, and inclusion—through the embrace and practice of my *Eight Habits of the Heart*, which are life lessons I learned from my original porch people, who lived them out in my presence and passed them along to me and now to you. They include a nurturing attitude, responsibility, dependability, friendship, brotherhood/sisterhood, high expectations, courage, and hope. These habits are not held captive by time and place. They are the essence of unselfishness lived out. When lived out, they reveal our better selves. They are just as much at home in your current workplace or learning place as they were for me in Glen Allan, Mississippi, decades ago.

To reap the benefits of respect, affirmation, and inclusion, you must commit to bringing these habits to life within every sphere of your influence on a daily basis. Tuck them in your briefcase. Take them to lunch. Make sure they are reflected in your various means of communication. Ensure that your conversations are well placed. This is not a project you can complete, then pat yourself on the back or hang a certificate of completion on your wall. It is a continuous process.

My porch people never tired of pouring their wisdom into my life. They showed me the importance of good relationships. Building and maintaining solid relationships is good business. And good business deserves a continuous, equally good process. Allocate the time to encourage such a process. Yes, you have the time to build this bridge—and to build it solidly. It will serve your vision well, whatever your vision might be. I know that you want 28/10: twenty-eight hours a day, ten days a week—more hours than allocated to take on this additional opportunity. But alas, like the rest of us, you will only have 24/7. Most entrepreneurs understand this and go out of their way to make sure they always take care of the people moving in and out of their lives in the time they have. This is an entrepreneurial thinking strategy and will have profound impact upon every area of your life including your embrace of innovation and starting your first business.

People matter, as do the relationships that you have the opportunity to build with them. Within the marketplace and just within life itself, this is a key success factor and an important element of entrepreneurial thinking. Remember, these strategies will all work in tandem to produce the desired end

Shift Your Thinking: Win where you stand

result: your success, wherever you stand. Entrepreneurs know this, and now so do you.

> *We don't accomplish anything in the world alone... and whatever happens is the result of the whole tapestry of one's life and all the weaving of individual threads from one to another that creates something.*
> —Sandra Day O'Connor, First female US Supreme Court Justice

Personal Questions to Ponder

Let's take a moment to reflect on where you feel you stand professionally and personally at this very moment.

1. As a professional, when and where did you first experience a culture where you felt you didn't matter? How did you respond?
2. Is building a solid relationship bridge important in your business? In your life? Do you see the relationship between building this bridge and the sustainability of your efforts?
3. How does RAI—respect, affirmation, and inclusion—look in your organization?
4. What have you done this week to build your solid relationship bridge?

Chapter 4

Slow Down to Lead

Slow down to lead, your fourth strategy, is not about stopping. Slow Down to Lead is about the allocation of your time and knowledge. This fourth strategy is about bringing others along and giving them an opportunity to actively and creatively participate. This is about recognizing and valuing others who will cross your path. It's also about realizing your strengths and what they can mean for someone else. This strategy is about being reflective, taking time to analyze, and planning your future with facts and good people on your side. It's about intentionally setting out to bring others along, wherever those others might be along your life or professional pathway. Slow down to lead is about not being afraid to trust others, and recognizing the importance of delegation. When leaders slow down to involve others, they are also setting an example of what is expected of those who follow.

Back home in the delta, I was made aware of "slowing down," although without all the explanation one would expect. Instead, decades later, I can still hear the voices of my porch people calling out to me, "Boy, you are walking so fast, you gonna outrun your own shadow." While growing up, I heard this all the time: "Boy, slow down!" I wasn't running. I wasn't even walking fast. But somehow they sensed those internal wheels turning faster and faster and moving me along to the point that I was missing valuable messages all around me and not providing conversation space to others. Now that I am older, I know they didn't mean "quit." My porch people just seemed to understand that you would miss some very important signals in life if you didn't slow down to be reflective and thoughtful. We know this to be true in our personal lives, but it is also true in our professional lives and in the marketplace where we work and study. This is even more important in today's marketplace where it is so easy to be caught up in a fast pace forward. We oftentimes mistake moving at warp speed as the trait needed to win. This is not so. At such speeds, relationships can be damaged, the very relationships you are trying to impress.

I found my porch people's admonition to slow down very valuable for me and for leadership in general. I have tried to follow that advice. As I study the well-known British entrepreneur Sir Richard Branson, I am excited that within his entrepreneurial world, he too has applied similar life lessons. It is obvious to me that he had his porch people as well. You will need yours also. Slowing down will give you the opportunity to recognize and value their voices in your life.

Branson, a British business magnate and investor, is best known as the founder and chairman of Virgin Group, a collection of more than four hundred companies. I chose Branson for this discussion because of his recognized leadership style—a style that includes slowing down on purpose. His teams are beneficiaries of his slowing down to lead. Maybe his leadership style can be partially attributed to his early childhood challenges—challenges that had the potential to sideline him. Instead, he shifted his thinking and actually began winning right where he stood. Branson was not always recognized by others as someone likely to succeed. As a young boy, he had dyslexia and performed poorly in school, but he also displayed

Shift Your Thinking: Win where you stand

the characteristics of an inventive mind. He was fortunate because his well-to-do parents were seemingly ahead of their time in encouraging him to not give up on himself and to put his dreaming into action—in effect, to win where he stood. I believe that their mentoring and support of his ideas played a great role in how he leads his companies today.

His leadership style seemed to favor the process of slowing down—a process that considers others. Such is necessary if you are to make decisions based on your assessments of the culture and the people who surround you. Being reflective is a direct benefit of slowing down and not "outrunning your shadow," as I was told. The process of slowing down allowed Branson to be reflective and to obtain the data and conversations needed to make the best decisions possible. This works for you as well. When you slow down, you can make better connections and experience the magic of your solid relationship bridge being built in your presence. For sustained success, it's important to be deliberate in keeping a pace that allows your team to keep up with you.

Leading your life or leading your company, this strategy will work well. Sir Richard Branson is very forthright in sharing what he learned and allowing us to look through his rearview mirror. In his interviews he speaks to the need to value and trust others, but to value and trust others requires knowing them. This does not happen automatically. Time and effort are required—hence the need to purposely slow down, even to the point of keeping a notepad with you to write down what others are saying and what you have promised.

Branson is known for doing this. Paying close attention to those around you is what he had witnessed in his parents, and early learning has long-range impact. Follow the timeless example given to Branson by his parents, who took the time to know their son, and who, when others said that he could possibly end up in prison, set out to harness his creativity in a positive fashion. Just like they did, when you get to know your people because you have slowed down, you are better positioned to know what is required of you to help maximize their potential. As Branson shared in his interview, knowing this information is critical in determining who will best fit in certain positions. And, I might add, your slowing down as a leader will also provide you the opportunity to discover those within your organizations who need mentoring. I would suggest that you lead the way in giving young talent that extra boost that your position and influence provides. This is a good model to consider. You don't have to hold a title and position to be a leader. Whenever you are charged to make something happen, your leadership of that charge kicks in.

Of course, it would seem that in the workplace, moving fast is the order of the day—not purposely slowing down. Sprinting does have its place on the running track, where rewards are given out to those who finish first. However, we are not talking about finish lines and personal trophies. We are not talking about being ahead of the pack. We are talking about leadership that embraces the vision and invites others to do likewise. This type of leadership that is reflective of a shift in thinking—entrepreneurial leadership. Leading is not about being out front with the plan and the authority, or about having a private parking space and giving orders to others. It's about example. It's about commitment. It's about accountability. It's about sustainability. It's about bringing other people along. Slow down to lead. You are being watched. Leading is about the signals being sent by the actions you take, and how those signals impact others. Entrepreneurs seem to be much aware of the power of their presence and most often try to maximize their influence in the best ways possible.

If you could take a quick trip over to England to visit one or several of Sir Richard's companies, you would find that his

Shift Your Thinking: Win where you stand

team is fully aware of his expectations. He has put in the time necessary to establish his example. This is what good leaders do. What do you want your team to see? What actions are you giving them to emulate? They will watch you. In the world of entrepreneurs, you are encouraged to take stock of the boss to learn how he or she thinks and to recognize what drives his or her actions. As a leader, you can bring this recognition into your life as positive action you want to embrace. As an employee, as a student, or a small business owner, your actions become your example. Wherever you are you can send a positive signal to someone else. In today's global environment, you will need a competitive edge; watching success and emulating what you observe could be that edge. Slowing down to an example is entrepreneurial thinking at work. Keep in mind, though, that if the leader is running so fast that his or her good attributes become a blur, he or she will be cheating those who are watching. Your signals as a leader are important. Clear and precise signals are best.

Thanks to advancing technology, your actions (good or bad) will oftentimes become the conversations that travel far beyond your business's walls. In the marketplace, being watched is par for the course. In any place where a hierarchy exists, people tend to look up. Those with positions and titles are watched. This rings true for all of us. It is so important to make sure that your walk and your talk are "kin to each other." This is another one of those sayings I picked up from my porch people. In the delta, "kinship" meant everything.

If you are a leader, whether just starting out or seasoned or just put in charge of the copy room, your position sends signals every single day. As an employee, you also send signals that tell the story of your commitment and dedication. If you are moving too fast, your signals might be blurred and misunderstood. When I say "slow down to lead," I am not asking you to come to a screeching halt. I am not asking you to stop in your tracks. I am asking you to take into consideration that if you get too far ahead of others on your team, you could create a relationship and information void. I also know that to move too fast is to sometimes overlook the reflection time needed, and to miss the data required to render good decisions or provide good reports. Twenty or more years ago, you would have had time to correct mistakes and smooth over bad decisions. Not today. Today requires being contemplative from the start and taking into consideration all of the compelling data. You will have to slow down to do this—hence the need to embrace a growth mind-set and to be determined while building a solid relationship bridge. These strategies work together, creating what we call entrepreneurial thinking.

When we read or listen to early stories of entrepreneurial success, we often find that the person who became the leader was not afraid to be an example of what was wanted and needed. Leading, as challenging as it is, is not an individual race. In your business, you are not rewarded for making it to the finish line before your team does. Take the opportunity to slow down and lead more effectively, sending the signals that really matter.

In the twenty-first-century workplace, unlike in the older pyramid leadership paradigm, this is not about one person as much as it is about the ability to assemble a team and the ability of the leader to create the culture needed to cultivate cohesion and collaboration. This seems to ring true among entrepreneurs. Cohorts and teams are commonplace in entrepreneurial environments, diverse groups working together to give life to new creative ideas. Trust plays a major role in such an environment. This comes across loud and clear in Sir Richard Branson's approach to leadership, as discussed in the 2013 Australian Institute of Management bulletin. Branson's approach is to set the standards and give his employees room to be partners in the process. Branson accepts his role as an example of the expectations. According to him, he trusts his people. He is not a micromanager.

You want to see your dream grow and exceed your expectations. This was also true in the Mississippi Delta when I was a young boy living with my great-aunt. I was definitely expected to exceed her expectations, which were high and demanding, and she gave me the room to do so. She was in all aspects a leader. She knew I was watching, and I saw her performance all my life and thoughtfully embraced the daily signals until I learned to expect excellence in myself. This way of leading in our house served me well when I was able to obtain work outside the house. I saw her live out her day in my presence. I was with her as she visited the sick. I can still see her sitting in her rocking chair by the front window writing letters to family and friends. I learned from her that "keeping in touch" mattered. Field work was hard, but I watched as she used her meager wherewithal to save for the future. She taught me to live for tomorrow, not just the day. Not a day goes by when I am not reminded of what I saw. When you slow down so that other can observe your actions, you are showing them the look and feel of your engagement and your commitment.

To this point, leadership is also about followership—the other people on the team and on the payroll, or the other side of the same coin, if you will. Leaders and followers are interdependent. If you have been defined as a leader but look behind you and find no followers, you've just been walking and talking to yourself. Productive followership should be your goal. This is what Sir Richard Branson wanted of his team. This is what my great-aunt wanted of me. As a leader, you should focus on the aspirations of those working with you. You should want them to thrive. To accept less is to minimize their value. As a member of the team, this should be your goal as well. However, such productive followership is not automatic. To achieve this type of followership, you must have thoughtful and reflective leadership in your place of business.

Productive followership is a direct result of intentional, people-focused leadership. It can even show up in the military, where following orders is the order of the day. In *The Art of Leadership: In the Footsteps of Giants,* author Raymond Yeh validated much of what I had heard from others regarding Herb Kelleher's leadership style—one where genuine concern for people is at the core of his decision making. Kelleher's Southwest Airlines is a testament to his leadership and people focus. According to Yeh, every excellent organization bears the stamp of its original leaders—those early visionaries. They intentionally set the standards, not just in wonderfully crafted memos, but through their daily actions and interactions. Such leadership is reflective and moving at warp speed is not the standard. Caring and respectful leadership is not held captive by a few well-known people. It's entrepreneurial thinking, but it's not a coded secret.

I specifically remember one such leader when I was a young airman stationed at Dow Air Force Base. I was young and still afraid, but I was determined to make this military venture work. After all, it was part of the journey that had started the day I won where I stood—the day I stopped trying to guess who was in the backseat of the Red Top Cab and began to see myself sitting there on my way to the rest of my life. Each victory of my "forward movement," no matter how small, was celebrated. And I kept looking for one more. For me, the military was "one more." The times were turbulent. The Viet Nam War was on all our minds. I had a job to do, but just like Mama Ponk, my great-aunt who raised me, I found a reason to be my best despite the

Shift Your Thinking: Win where you stand

surrounding circumstances. I saw one more opportunity there to demonstrate excellence.

I was able to do so because I had discovered a quality of military leadership I had not expected: the captain who commanded our area was thoughtful and reflective. This was demonstrated in the way he approached those of us who reported to him. He valued our shared humanity and in doing so set the examples we needed to see and follow.

In your workplace, even though employees may have signed on voluntarily, their productive followership is neither automatic nor guaranteed. Entrepreneurs seem to know that their actions matter. They seem to understand that they are being watched. Their pace is critical. If they move too fast, they might just miss out on ideas and suggestions from others. Slowing down to lead gives you the opportunity to value the presence of your team and their input. Listening takes place as the pace slows down. To win in your marketplace, you need your team's commitment. You will need to give your team a reason to commit and follow through.

As Sir Richard Branson said, "Other people have ideas also." Plan to listen and to create a culture that welcomes bright, new ideas. Today your team's value extends far beyond blindly following orders. Your team members are indeed your partners. The entrepreneurial thinker embraces this concept. Even in the air force, where top-down leadership was the norm, my captain left us with the opinion that we were partners in the War effort. I embraced what I saw and experienced of his leadership.

I also embraced what I saw and experienced of my great-grand father's leadership. Again, I return to one of my porch people, Poppa Joe, my great-grandfather who held an informal leadership position in the community. I saw him intentionally slow down to engage with others. I was there as he reached out when I thought we should have been doing something else.

However, as a kid growing up, I watched my great-grandpa intently—this balding black man with twinkles in his eyes. On Saturdays, the two of us would take a ride to Greenville, Mississippi, then known as the Queen City of the Delta. It was during those rides in his 1949 Buick that Poppa's thoughtful and productive leadership became clear. I saw him use his informal position as a community leader to involve and reach out to others as he intentionally slowed down—literally—for them. I always cringed when Poppa slowed down, because I knew that some type of change was about to take place. This man valued people.

We both saw Mr. Fields walking right down the middle of the road. I tried to pretend that I had not noticed him. I knew what to expect next: the car almost coming to a complete stop as this weary hitchhiker was invited to ride with us. Poppa booted me off the front seat, where I had been extremely comfortable. I didn't like it, but later I realized that I had not been born in the front seat and that sharing with others took nothing from my life. I think Poppa understood that he was being watched by his young great-grandson. Over time, I took what I saw to heart, and it continues to serve me well today. I learned that other people matter and that I have time to share from my life. I have time to slow down. Had this ordinary man who was also an extraordinary leader not slowed down, I would have missed very valuable lessons. I was booted to the back seat, but looking back, I realize it's much more fun having someone in the Red Top Cab along with you.

Several years ago, when consulting for Lockheed Martin, I was invited to a leadership dinner with the opportunity to hear firsthand from Bob Stevens, the CEO at the time. I was excited. Most often, a visiting consultant is not a guest at such an event. I was fortunate to be invited and to hear his talk. Stevens gave a dynamic presentation, laying out all the strengths and capabilities of the company.

Shift Your Thinking: Win where you stand

However, at the end of his talk, his presentation shut down, and not a sound could be heard anywhere. He walked out into the audience of his assembled leadership team. I was at a back table with a good view, and I watched as he focused on each one of his leaders who had come in from around the world. I still remember his nine captivating words: "Your people will do what they see you do." In that simple but powerful statement, he also implied that he was aware of each of them watching him. That was nearly a decade ago. I still reference that dinner whenever I can. He was absolutely right: people look up to get their cues. If you are moving too fast, the cues might be missed or misunderstood.

Be willing to slow down. Be willing to be reflective and analytical. Be willing to bring others along. These three actions will help you to both plan and act based on good strategic data. Move too fast, and you may end up missing important conversations, overlooking strategic partnerships and potentially harming the very relationships you are out to build.

It's better to put in the work required on the front end rather than have to go back and reconstruct what has broken down. To do so is to lose valuable time out of your 24/7—the time frame that we all have to get it done. Time is a valuable gift. Use it wisely.

It is in the slowing-down process that you fine-tune the leadership skills necessary to rally your team to the vision. Remember, your vision statement is an important document. It was not meant to merely be a wall decoration. It expresses your purpose and gives room for others to join you in making the vision come to life.

Take the time to get to know the people that populate your life (your business associates, the students you teach, etc.) and to send signals that will keep them engaged and committed. This will have far-reaching and long-lasting benefits, leading to what we call succeeding in the twenty-first-century marketplace—where we live, work, study, and play.

Slowing down to lead is a great strategy to leverage and a great example to leave for others to follow and emulate. Those in leadership positions should never shy away from being the example they wish to see in others. And if you are an intern, employee on your career path or a student, it's good to know this now and to start the process early on of shaping your leadership for sustained success. Embrace the growth mind-set. Be determined. Understand the value of slowing down to lead—giving other the opportunity to see you in action and learn during the process. Successful entrepreneurial thinkers in all walks of life have left us the proof support that slowing down to lead is a strategy worth embracing. It's all about shifting your thinking and winning where you stand.

Example is not the main thing influencing others, it's the only thing.
—Dr. Albert Schweitzer, noted musician, medical missionary to Africa, and winner of the 1952 Nobel Peace Prize

Shift Your Thinking: Win where you stand

Personal Questions to Ponder

Let's take a moment to reflect on where you feel you stand professionally and personally at this very moment.

1. How often do you stop to reflect and analyze the situation before starting the execution process?
2. How much time are you willing to put in to ensure productive followership?
3. Throughout your career, how would you value the impact of the signals you've received?
4. What traits do you possess that will cause others to want to follow your lead?

Chapter 5

Know Your Business "Health" Metrics

There's an old saying in business that you can only improve that which you measure. It makes sense that, if you set a goal to improve your performance or grow your revenue, you must keep track of how you're doing to know if you're moving toward that goal.
—John Jantsch, author, speaker, and small-business marketing consultant

Knowing Your Business "health" metrics is a very important entrepreneurial thinking strategy. It's about paying attention to the details and being fully aware of what is required of you and your team to stay on top of your plan. Knowing the "health" metrics of your business is about valuing and owning the managerial and operational decisions you've made. Metrics direct strategic actions—manageable actions. Metrics are used to drive success through improvements and to help focus the team and the resources on what's important. It's about the details and how they are managed. Stories from entrepreneurs who did not keep their eyes on the details often tell how they barely escaped failure by taking their eyes off the ball. However, knowing and sharing the importance of paying attention to details is what most successful entrepreneurs do. Early on, their metrics might not be formalized, but of great value nonetheless. These entrepreneurs know what has to take place on a daily basis. They show up early. They leave late. They have no desire to fail. And of course, we want success for you and your endeavors; thus this strategy. By keeping track of the details—the health of the business on a consistent basis, standards are also set for others to see and follow. You must determine your metrics and how best to bring them forward. Having metrics is about not leaving things to chance, as well as setting the stage for accountability.

Asking questions and probing for answers is not about not trusting as some might think. This is what you do if you want to ensure success. Valuing commitment and accountability is about asking questions. If you have built a solid relationship bridge, the questioning will not be seen as invasive, but welcomed. Entrepreneurs just want to know the details in order to not be caught off guard and to better handle their respective tasks. We should all want this regardless of how we define ourselves. The more information we have, the better our ability to deal with the challenges and the opportunities we might face. Entrepreneurs also want their people to know the details of the business, as well as how all the parts fit together. Knowing the details and being able to fit all the moving parts together is part of entrepreneur success. But it is not a secret.

In business, total market awareness is the goal, rather than just knowing your specific area of responsibility, as the latter leads to being unable to successfully connect across business lines. No matter where you are at the moment, knowing the full picture will serve you well, as will knowing what it will take to keep you moving in a positive direction. This strategy is also about knowledge. Knowledge is power. And shared knowledge takes it to the next level.

Whether one is just starting out in business, a seasoned businessperson, or a student at that proverbial crossroad, these entrepreneurial strategies support the importance of knowing the business "health" metrics as they play out in our life and work. To answer the following questions, you must know what's going on both in your business and in your life. So as a starter, let's consider the six questions below:

1) **Is your business performing well?**
2) **Are you making money?**
3) **Are you losing money?**
4) **Are your customers being treated properly?**
5) **What are the variances from the plan?**
6) **Do you actually have a plan?**

The value you place on these questions and the answers required will determine how you structure your staff meetings and how employees respond going forward. If you are meeting the plan, your meetings will be positive and focused on supporting the team as it continues moving from good to great. However, if the standards within the plan are not being met, and such is clearly shown through the analysis of the published metrics, it's time to ask why and to reemphasize the expectations for each person according to the plan. This type of analysis has value professionally and personally.

Thoughtfully focusing on the plan entails attention to the details. This is about commitment and accountability to a set of established expectations. These two qualities are not entrepreneur specific. Entrepreneur or not, neither of the two works if you are not willing to have your efforts measured and to gain the knowledge required to successfully complete your tasks. Your response to know what's going on and doing what is required becomes your commitment. Without

Shift Your Thinking: Win where you stand

measurements, there's little or no accountability. And without metrics, there's nothing to measure. Back home in the delta, this was clearly understood, though expressed differently. Cousin Sister always said, "Everbody needs a pattern to cut by." Cousin Sister was my Mama Ponk's first cousin. They were sister and brother children. I have no idea how she came to be called Cousin Sister. Her birth name was Savannah. Anyway, having a pattern was her way of understanding the value of metrics. She simply boiled it down to what she understood—a pattern. Without an established and acceptable pattern, you will not know if you are inside or outside the line. Giving this type of strategic attention to workplace details may not be the fun part of the business, but it is most definitely an essential part of its long-term success. In the workplace, we need our defined patterns, as it were. And according to Cousin Sister, our lives deserve a pattern as well.

Your life metrics and business metrics are intertwined. It's difficult to run a good business when your personal life is out of sync. *At the end of the day, the embrace of metrics is about the entire team being committed and accountable. If the team is only one person, as it was when I first started out in business, the same level of commitment and accountability applies.*

The competitiveness of the twenty-first-century marketplace demands this high level of commitment and accountability. No one can afford to assume that the key drivers of the business are being monitored. This knowledge is too important to be left to a guess. Conversations must be held. Again, it's important to create a culture where accepting responsibility for the vision which encompasses all the moving parts is the norm. "This is not my responsibility" is an unacceptable response. Succeeding is the responsibility of each employee. If you don't fully understand your business's operating parts, then it becomes very difficult to know how to stay on top of the operational process and how to hold yourself and others accountable for your and their actions.

A story in the September 2013 issue of *Forbes Life* examined the successful life of Tommy Hilfiger. What I found interesting about him was that he displayed an entrepreneurial mind-set early on as a teenager, and he had the stories to prove it. This was so meaningful to me, as I embrace the notion of "winning where you stand" at whatever age and time in life. Having this early onset of a growth mind-set will enable you to weather the storms that will surely come, as they did for this young entrepreneur. At age twenty-five, extraordinarily successful, he had to file for bankruptcy. His success was spiraling downward. In his words, "I was embarrassed. I had started with nothing and worked so hard, and we were close to making it really big, but I had taken my eyes off the ball. I believed that the business would just continue to do well."

Whether it's Hilfiger's business or your own, you must pay attention to the business of the business, or else you might find yourself in a similar situation. The good news is that this failure did not shut him down. True, he had taken his eyes off the ball—the day-to-day attention to detail that matters—but his mind-set served him well. He recovered, and the rest is history. His lessons are obvious: Know every aspect of what it takes to keep moving your projects ahead. Be personally committed to the tasks required. Keep your head, heart and hands in the daily mix. Make the mix practical. Keep a daily log of all you have promised to do and all you have done. Review your day at the end of the day so that you will have a better sense of how to face your tomorrow. Keep your word to yourself. And keep your word to others.

This is the type of thinking, responsive action, and commitment you can bring into your own life. Like those successful entrepreneurs, you too can accept this role of accountability,

Shift Your Thinking: Win where you stand

which brings with it a sense of ownership—a shift in thinking that is so important in today's marketplace. And further, these very important operational details should be communicated to all team members, whether the team is only one other person or more. This is the thinking that successful entrepreneurs put into practice. Within their world, such daily responsiveness becomes part of the process. Such action will serve you well in business and in life.

In terms of individual physical health, we have an array of things that must be measured against predetermined, published standards. For example, we know what our heart rate and pulse should read, and what our body temperature and blood pressure should be. The standards have been set, and because we know how to check them, we know what actions to take to correct the situation, if need be. It is no different in our professional workplaces. ***If we are to stay ahead of the curve and succeed in the marketplace, we need to know the health metrics of the company.*** You need to know those predetermined standards. Are they concise and meaningful? Is everyone aware of the actions required of them to ensure that the standards are being met? Where are the metrics posted? And are you making this an ongoing conversation, always keeping the metrics top of mind? Every member of the team needs to be knowledgeable and involved in ensuring the standards are set and being met. This is one conversation that should take place on a daily basis, fully utilizing all the tools of communication you have available. Cousin Sister knew this in Glen Allan. She knew we needed a guideline to live our lives well. And so it is with our professional endeavors.

Good performance on a consistent basis is necessary to maintain the good health of the business. It's important to know the performance metrics of your business and how well the team is carrying them out. Entrepreneurs are quick to point out that they have no problem making sure that their teams are fully aware of what has to be done daily and hourly to ensure sustainable success. Within businesses, such conversations of inquiry should start in the interview process and continue throughout the career journey.

This strategy that highlights the value of knowing the details and embracing metrics has value across the business spectrum. Let's go back to Saint Louis for a minute to the mid-1960s. In Saint Louis on Spring Street, right down form the old Busch Baseball Stadium, Uncle Madison had a small confectionary which served as a neighborhood grocery, and a notions store. It was his small version of the Walmart neighborhood grocery store. He was not well educated, but he knew every aspect of his business. He reminded me of my uncle from back home. I knew I could learn from him. So I started voluntarily working for him and was eventually hired. At the end of each day, I would watch him as he checked on every item in the store. He knew what had been sold and what remained. He would laughingly ask his customers, "How's the boy doing?" I would listen as I received glowing reports—which I knew I would. We would all laugh, but looking back some forty years later, I realize that Uncle Madison had his metrics: his inventory, a balanced cash drawer, and the comments from his customers. It really hasn't changed. Success depends on knowing what is expected, having known guidelines and proceeding to follow through on them. I was young, but committed and accountable for my actions. I took ownership of that small opportunity provided me at Uncle Madison's small store. Uncle Madison and his customers were the beneficiaries. My actions made a difference. It also established my own sense of being responsible and dependable. People wanted to stop by Brazier's Confectionary, passing several others along the way. To remain competitive and be successful, both organizations and people will need to

Shift Your Thinking: Win where you stand

reflect this sense of ownership. Accepting ownership of your opportunity is embedded in organizations where entrepreneurial thinking is embraced. Uncle Madison also called entrepreneurial thinking and response, gumption. Because I displayed a sense of ownership and no detail was too small for me to handle. He said I had gumption. Uncle Madison was an entrepreneur—an ordinary man with limited education, roadblocks and barriers, but displayed gumption on a daily basis. He knew the ins and outs of his small business and expected the same of me. I didn't let him down.

When I listened to those who, along with me were being inducted into SMEI, I recall their talk about the nuts and bolts of their businesses and how they attributed their success to paying close attention to every detail. They had their pattern to follow and for others to replicate. They were the owners. They were the first dreamers. They were the passengers in their Red Top Cabs. However, for others to join in—becoming accountable and committed, a culture has to be in place so that each member of the team feels a sense of ownership and are also willing to connect with others to ensure corporate success—the embrace of effective metrics. To create this culture of ownership and pride is to foster an entrepreneurial way of thinking throughout the organization—a way of thinking that says, "I get the vision. I accept my responsibility to help bring it to reality. I get great personal satisfaction from a job well done. I know this to be important—even more so today, as competitive forces appear regularly."

I want you to take a minute and think seriously about the quote below. It is taken from an excerpt of an open letter from Dr. John Sullivan, internationally recognized HR consultant from Silicon Valley, to Mark Zuckerberg, CEO of Facebook, and Larry Page, CEO of Google, entitled "Avoid the 'Great to Good' Downward Spiral," dated April 23, 2012.

"In a start-up, it is obvious to everyone what is important. However, as an organization gets larger, it's common to overly rely on the corporate culture to communicate your message about the importance of performance, innovation, speed, and calculated risk taking. Because "what you measure and what you reward...gets done," your cultural message must be unambiguously reinforced on a daily basis through your measurement, reporting, and reward processes."

Again the need to know and measure comes to the forefront as part of a business's sustainable success factors. Even at such places as Facebook and Google, relationships play an important role in the continued execution of this type of thinking. It's essential to know what's going on in your department, at your desk, and in the business. The health and wellness of your business is closely tied to the culture that surrounds the team. The entrepreneurial way of thinking is not just for the person who brings a new product to market. It is also a valuable asset for those who have to design, build, test, and deliver it to the market. This way of thinking brings with it a sense of ownership regardless of the level of involvement, as well as personal pride in a job or a task well done.

Lessons learned from employing and adhering to good metrics are mobile. They are not held captive by time and place. I saw this in Glen Allan when I was Mr. Walter's are water boy—a job so far removed from what I do today, but impactful nonetheless. Mr. Walter's business was transporting the field hands to work each day, and I had the job of supplying that much-needed water—ice-cold and timely. Those were my two metrics. I had to be alert and ready and fully aware of time allocation. The environment was not the best, and the field hands' work was backbreaking, but Mr. Walter insisted on excellence from me and his expectations had already been established. I was the one bright spot in their day. I couldn't let them down. It

Shift Your Thinking: Win where you stand

would have been so easy to let the surroundings dictate my level of excellence. Yet I chose to think and respond differently. It was the right thing to do. Even though the environment was not exciting or memorable, the metrics were known. I did my job. I was timely. The water was ice cold. Those around me were well served. They were both our customers. They had choices, but showed up at his truck each day.

Customer loyalty is just as important today and even more so when so many options exist. Maintaining market share is important to companies. Gone are the days when business owners could safely assume that their customers were theirs forever. While you are sleeping, the competition is gearing up to increase their market share, which means seeing a decrease in yours. To this point, tending to the "health and wellness" of the company becomes increasingly important. In 2012, I had an opportunity to talk with a division manager of an international company about this very same issue. He was taking a close look at his company's worldwide market share and at what he felt needed to be taking place in the aerospace manufacturing business. He wanted to develop entrepreneurial thinking managers who embraced the established metrics of the company. He requested a workshop to point out the value of such thinking to any company and to theirs in particular.

Individual actions matter at every level and within all departments. Publishing metrics to which the entire team is accountable is your key to quality performance and sustainable outcomes. Such collaborative responsiveness shows up early in many start-ups due to their lack of ready cash, which oftentimes forces team members to embrace a sense of ownership as well as partnership. Yet such actions, loaded with positive consequences, are worthy of embrace beyond those start-up days, even if a major player in the aerospace industry.

Clifton L. Taulbert

The term "health metrics" is used to focus your attention on the fact that a company can be sick or well. To tend to the health of the business is to embrace accountability at all levels and to be detail focused—not unlike entrepreneurs who are known for closely watching all the performance elements that are important to their success. The rumor is that Oprah watches everything. I don't know this to be fact, but I am aware of her monumental success. Sam Walton often showed up unannounced and could be seen walking his aisles—looking over his products and listening to his customers. They both were looking based on their expectations—their metrics. Was it necessary? Look at their entrepreneurial success and let that be your answer. Entrepreneurs are invested in their outcomes; such commitment can also be called pride of ownership, an attribute that is often assigned to entrepreneurs and their attention to details. However, this does not mean that this attribute is inaccessible to you as an employee, an intern, student in search of your destiny, or a budding entrepreneur. To embrace such an attitude is to adhere to the growth mind-set that leads to the entrepreneurial thinking you admire. The need to have an accountable workforce where the metrics matter and the needed supporting culture are not independent of each other. After all, they are the team to move you to the next level of success.

As the CEO of African Bean Company—the home of Roots Java Coffee—I am more than aware of the need to draw upon entrepreneurial thinking to make this venture a success. My team must understand the metrics. And I have to intentionally build the necessary supporting culture. My Tulsa team must be kept informed on what is required of them. Our relationship with our roasting company has to be a priority. Our communication strategy has to be in place. Our concern ranges from the fluctuating commodities market to shipping across the Atlantic. Bills must be paid on time and pickups and deliveries made on

Shift Your Thinking: Win where you stand

schedule. I need each member of our small team committed and accountable. We are too small to drop the ball. I am committed to holding strategic, informative and probing staff meetings when I don't feel like doing so. These meetings have become part of how we do business. Knowledge and information must be shared at all levels. I have to lead from a growth mind-set perspective. Our metrics span from the country of Rwanda to the FedEx shipping location down the street. To have a team displaying pride in effort is to have this much-desired ownership mentality. This is what we strive to have and is so important to the embrace of our "health" metrics. Just remember to create this sense of ownership at all levels where metrics are welcomed, the culture you create and sustain becomes important.

Your people will do what they see you do. They will listen to what you say and discuss with others what they heard, but your actions are the signals that really matter.

Culture matters. It matters within all our places. Within an engaging and unselfish culture, you will be better positioned to bring the importance of this strategy into your personal and professional lives, farther experiencing the impact of entrepreneurial thinking. Knowing and adhering to the metrics is essential to ensure this branding. This makes for good business. And can also positively impact your life's journey.

An empowered organization is one in which individuals have the knowledge, skill, desire, and opportunity to personally succeed in a way that leads to collective organizational success.
—Stephen R. Covey, author of *The Seven Habits of Highly Successful People*

Personal Questions to Ponder

Let's take a moment to reflect on where you feel you stand professionally and personally at this very moment.

1. What are the health and wellness metrics of your company?
2. Where are they published, and how often are they discussed?
3. How do you reward your team when these metrics are met and exceeded?
4. Do you feel that having an "ownership" perspective is an effective asset in your personal journey?

Chapter 6

Be Prepared to Swim Upstream!

Be Prepared to swim Upstream is the sixth strategy that further reveals the inside of entrepreneurial thinking. You will need this strategy in the marketplace, and in your life. Easy is not guaranteed in either place! It never has been although sometimes, it can look that way on paper. In the real world, however, where you live, work, study and play, stuff happens, unplanned and unexpected. At this point, the swim upstream becomes the option. It's not an easy option, nor is it a planned option. However, the unplanned and the unexpected can bring a new and positive reality. Negative challenges can certainly hurl us upstream, but also unexpected and unplanned success.

We will all have this story of having to swim upstream one time or another in our life. However, we celebrate entrepreneurs because despite their swimming upstream due to a negative event, they refuse to give up. They flex new muscles and focus. Their growth mind-set drives them toward victory. This is what I want for each of you—to understand that the swim upstream can be the turn-around that keeps you turned around and winning. Hilfiger had to stop midstream and reassess his journey. Herb Kelleher and his Southwest Airlines team had to stop midstream multiple times. Despite Oprah's monumental success with her incredible talk show, OWN—her network—required that she stop midstream and do an assessment, getting a new focus and new partners. Life is not easy! Entrepreneurs know that innovation is not easy and can cost more in time, money and talent than originally planned, and despite the newscasters counting them out, they continue upstream in a different direction and more often than not achieve their goals. Their lessons of tenacity and vision serve all of us well. To swim upstream requires vision and tenacity and more, and our will to continue that swim upstream is bolstered by those who have gone before us.

Swimming upstream is just plain hard, but oftentimes necessary. The salmon make it look easy, but I can assure you that they use an internal guiding system. I would venture to say that in this upstream process, they use muscles not required when swimming downstream with the current on their side while basking in the expected and acceptable normal. That trek upstream is not something that we want to happen, whether brought on by incredible growth or a major disaster. Either way it might be part of the journey that we will eventually define as a successful one. Once headed upstream, we engage new strategies and we focus more intently. We are also not so easily distracted. Again, your mind-set matters. You need the growth mind-set that refuses to give up when things are not going the way you planned. The fixed mind-set, on the other hand, has little tolerance for challenge. It's a comfortable mind-set. With that mind-set, giving up and walking away can become the easy option. Or you can call in a team of experts and bring fresh eyes and ideas to issues at hand. To stand still or give up is not what I want for myself or you. It would have been so easy to simply dream about life in the backseat of the Red Top Cab. At the time, being a passenger in the Red Top Cab was close to an impossibility. Fortunately, I chose to think that the impossible is possible. I wanted more. I am so

Shift Your Thinking: Win where you stand

grateful I chose to make my dreaming my reality. It all started with the shift in my thinking and the acceptance of a mind-set that was future focused. I was still swimming upstream, still surrounded by legal segregation and still picking cotton. But my mind was now susceptible to new ideas and bigger dreams.

To not give up is the growth mind-set in action. The turning point happens when we turn the awkward move into what looks to others like a well-orchestrated dance. What still resonates with me from the night I was inducted into the SMEI Academy of Achievement are the inductees' stories of the awkward and unexpected moments that demanded more than they thought they had, and that eventually gave them more than they expected. When you don't quit, you will discover so much about your skills, abilities, and creativity. Sometimes this swim upstream will take you to a celebration that, without it, would not have happened. More than mere words, embracing this strategy is indeed powerful.

On June 27, 2014, I found myself in such a place of celebration—a celebration of the awesome power of what can happen when the growth mind-set is chosen and entrepreneurial thinking becomes a way of life. I was invited to offer the keynote address at the dedication of the Nate Waters Physical Therapy Center in downtown Tulsa. Mr. Waters had passed away, but his entrepreneurial spirit while swimming upstream had given birth to this new Tulsa Community College facility. The grounds were filled with Tulsans from all walks of life, who had all come to not only welcome the center, but to pay homage to this great entrepreneurial spirit. He was known for being doggedly persistent and for embracing tenacity and being visionary as a way of life.

In the midst of our celebration of this entrepreneur was the other reality: he won when he should have quit. Nate Waters was not a long-distance runner. He was not known as a college jock or as a contender for the Heisman Trophy. Yet this young entrepreneur had tapped into the growth mind-set and embraced an entrepreneurial way of thinking. His thinking had taken him and all of us to another level of expectation of ourselves. On the day of the dedication, Nate Waters was hailed by Thomas McKeon, the president of TCC, as an Oklahoma hero. Nate's definitive embrace of the growth mind-set and his application of entrepreneurial thinking to his life had caught the attention of the well-known oil baron, Boone Pickens. They had become lifelong friends—this African American paraplegic and the Texas oil baron. They met while Nate was swimming upstream focused and determined. The oil baron admired the strokes Nate was making and found reason to join this remarkable young man.

As I prepared my talk, all I could imagine was that Nate Waters ran so fast, we forgot he was wheelchair bound. His spirit stood so tall, we had to look up to see his winsome smile. This entrepreneurial thinker brought us into his big vision, not his physical limitations. There were so many things about his life that spoke to the power of entrepreneurial thinking and being prepared to swim upstream. Nate should not have graduated from college, but he did. He should not have been a community activist, but he was. He should not have vocally advocated for those with disabilities, but he did. He should not have had friends in the highest of places, but he had them. He should have been discouraged and angry: life had dealt him a deck of cards that would be difficult for anyone to play and win. Yet instead of giving in to a fixed mind-set, which would have been easy to do and on some level understandable, he smiled and made his life one of service to others. He won where he stood. And we cheered.

In a wheelchair or on a cotton row in the Mississippi Delta, we have the capacity to stand and win where we are. It never happens automatically—hence the importance of the right

Shift Your Thinking: Win where you stand

mind-set choice to keep you pushing or picking toward your dream. Nate Waters' story is proof of what can happen if we are willing to shift our thinking and embrace this visionary way of living our lives as entrepreneurial thinkers. Challenges are not eradicated with such a perspective, but your will to win remains the focus and your choice of mind-set the driver.

Easy had not been guaranteed for Nate Waters. But he took Voltaire at his word and decided how he would play the cards dealt him in order to win the game. In fact, his whole life, from age nineteen to thirty-five, when he died in 2013, was filled with swimming upstream against the natural flow of the current. His upstream swim is what we watched as his entrepreneurial thinking kept him saying to himself and others, "I can do this! I will do this!"

Nate Waters was a not a stranger to me, but someone I knew and admired. Early on we had met and explored the possibility of writing his life story, but we never got around to doing so because he was always too busy to be in one place long enough. The wheelchair had to get used to him. I was honored and humbled to speak at this entrepreneur's departure to another life. I remember hearing Sam Combs, another Oklahoma entrepreneur and from the Oklahoma oil industry, make this comment: "I tell you he never gave you a chance to focus on his wheelchair. Before I could ask how he was doing, he was reaching out his hand to me and asking the state of my life—Sam how are you doing." To swim upstream is not what we request, but the unplanned and the unexpected show up without invitation being extended. However, choosing the right mind-set and embracing a transformative way of thinking can indeed take you into your destiny—a destiny that can be so powerful that a wheelchair-bound young man could have the attention of common folk like me and oil barons like Boone Pickens. Nate Waters shifted his thinking and won *big* right where he stood, and he brought us all along. Is this not what we admire? Is this not what we want for ourselves and others—a life that ultimately makes a difference? Entrepreneurial thinking provides us this opportunity. Its' how we play the game, however, that determines the look of the winning.

If Nate Waters could swim upstream and master his marketplace, so can all of us. Winning in our marketplace, right where we are, is what we want, and the plan is to make it happen. We have the right mind-set. We are determined. Our relationship bridge is solid. We are people focused, and we know the nuts and bolts of our work. Even so, "stuff" happens. Somewhere along the way, we are hit square in the face with reality—such as a debilitating spinal cord injury at nineteen. The unplanned and unexpected show up as problems and disturbing news most often not of our making. We can walk away, or we can deal with it. It is our choice. We can lower our heads and tuck our tails between our legs, or we can follow the salmon upstream, so to speak. Just remember that your move matters!

I've often wondered Nate's dream for himself before the injury that changed his life. We do have those times when it seems as if all the stars are aligned and we can make no mistakes. Our conversations with family and friends are all future-focused as they should be. We are being applauded on all sides and right in the **middle of the stream, headed downstream toward "happy hour." Then, suddenly, what was easy seeming easy and going our way disappears and nothing is working the way you planned. Instead of happy hour, you are now faced with both late hours and early hours**. Continuing downstream—embracing the current processes that aren't working—is not the answer. The problems mount in that direction. Frustration mounts. Internal conversations become focused on questioning everything. Nate Waters' life is saying, "Don't panic." If you are finding yourself at this place, I am also saying,

Shift Your Thinking: Win where you stand

now is not the time to panic and quit. Entrepreneurs face this all the time. The decisions they make become the conversations we hold about their success. They put on the brakes, pivot, and turn upstream—taking a different approach. They marshal their time to embrace and put in place that new approach.

Remember Nate Waters? He refused to let his paralysis define his life. He refused to let the wheelchair limit his mobility. At nineteen, life hurled him upstream, and he dealt with it in our presence.

Remember Tommy Hilfiger? Well, at twenty-five he also learned that easy is not guaranteed. He had to swim upstream and bring a level of focus to his work that early on he had not embraced. According to Hilfiger, however, his failure was his best lesson. Rather than quit, he doubled his efforts and sharpened his focus, becoming "hyper-focused," as described in the article. He analyzed what had gone right and what had gone wrong and proceeded to establish the pattern of thinking that continues today to serve him and his company well. He didn't quit.

Entrepreneurs often have reasons to throw in the towel, but they don't. Too much time, energy, and creativity have been invested to quit. Their internal vision of their success continues to guide their actions. No time for a night out with the crew. No time for distractions. It's time to move from being emotionally paralyzed. It is time for action.

What things went right? This is the first question you must ask yourself while in swimming upstream. It's important to know that even though easy has disappeared, all of your efforts have not been wasted. So write down what you did right and what worked.

Take a breather and go to the next crucial step. What went wrong? Oops! It's all right to be at this place. It's important to jot down what went wrong as well. You'll need both lists when you move into the comparative analysis mode. In the close look at what went wrong, you sometimes make positive discoveries for the future. Did you see red flags and ignore them? It's easy to do, especially if it seems that all is well. Most times in those cases, the red flags of warning are treated like flies. You just want to swat them away and move on, rather than embrace their warning and take the time to investigate. Investigation might cut into happy hour or those nice distractions.

Writing down what went right and what went wrong prepares you to bring in the assistance needed to put you back on a winning path. It also highlights your next move. Maybe now you will have a better picture of your strengths and weaknesses. This upstream process takes you out of the rush to be seen as successful and into the reality of making sure you are doing what it takes to be and remain successful.

This is entrepreneurial thinking: facing your reality head-on and embracing the mind-set to get you on the road to your dreams. This is not the time to put your head in the sand. Swimming upstream—dealing with challenges while gaining new perspectives and establishing new survival guidelines—is the alternative. The lives of entrepreneurs tell us that we are not the only people who have had to swim upstream, and it's important to bring these success stories into your life. Entrepreneurs are real people, and their real stories will serve to inspire you, becoming in many instances that much-needed life jacket, or the will to not be overcome by the unplanned success. Unplanned and unexpected is the culprit. It can show up on either side of the ledger. The success strategies of the entrepreneurs we celebrate for whatever reason are not secrets. However, their success can motivate you, but the next move is up to you. Swimming upstream may not have been in your plan, but it has now become your opportunity. It is this recognition and positive response, wherever you are in life, which will set you apart.

Shift Your Thinking: Win where you stand

In the marketplace and in life, things don't always go as planned. Your mind-set matters!

However, after leaving the delta after high school graduation, Saint Louis was not as I had dreamed. As smart as I thought I was, I was unable to land a job. I had to take care of myself, and this reality had not been part of my planning. I had no other choice than swim upstream. Swimming upstream is when I took notice that my uncle Madison could use extra help in his small store. During those months, I developed people skills and learned how to save money in a way that would serve me well throughout my life.

When Herb Kelleher and his partner, Rollin King, decided to enter the airline industry, they had not factored in the massive amount of opposition they would face. So instead of immediately getting their airline off the ground, they found themselves involved in continuous court battles for years. They faced legal hassles and personal frustration, but they refused to quit. They were entrepreneurs, and quitting was not their option. They couldn't go forward, so they regrouped and headed upstream and discovered new pathways.

During their swim upstream, they developed a creative focus and strategic perspective that could very well have otherwise eluded them. By 1971, after more than three years of court battles, they were in the air and gaining the reputation of "outside of the box" thinking. None of us want the hassle and the challenges that come our way, but once the cards are in our hands, we must decide how we will play the game. This is what we admire in those we celebrate as successful entrepreneurs.

This swim upstream is natural for salmon but can be awkward at best for humans. Yet we know that when the unexpected happens, we have a choice. We can continue downstream even though productivity has almost come to a dead stop, or we can learn from others who saw the red flags and turned against the tide. Continuing this movement downstream—doing what you have always done and know how to do—requires little or no effort. You know the territory. Happy-hour friends are plentiful. The workload may not be producing what you want or need, but you are comfortable. The fixed mind-set loves "comfortable" because no effort is required, and courage to move forward is not needed.

On the other hand, swimming upstream and dealing with the unplanned issues at hand will no doubt take you out of the mainstream you know so well. Courage is required as you set out to find a new circle of friends and advisors—those who will be there to help maneuver you through the challenges, wherever you might find yourself. Swimming upstream successfully will in fact require a lifeline of people who see themselves in your vision. When Nate faced his darkest hours, he had to reach out to others—many who were not from his neighborhood, and because of his mind-set and his way of thinking about his life, the others reached back, and he found himself being embraced by friends who were willing to become his lifeline.

Entrepreneurial thinking will enable you to embrace this time rather than seeing it as the time to step off the field of play. This is why such thinking is so important to sustained success. Entrepreneurs—those who have gone through times of doubt, lack of funds, and sleepless nights—understand that having to swim upstream is most often just a natural part of succeeding in the marketplace and in life.

What can an upstream journey look like in the marketplace for ordinary people like me and you? It could be losing your job through a layoff or a merger. A business partnership could go sour. It could also be an unexpected promotion with unexpected strings. You could have this bright idea, but be afraid to step out. I assure you that many of us will have our day of swimming upstream. However, once we have in fact pivoted

Shift Your Thinking: Win where you stand

and turned upstream, our response is all that matters at that point. The cards are in our hands.

Even though the Red Top Cab has taken me on a journey way beyond my imagination, swimming upstream has been a continuous part of my life. I had to swim upstream several times, and I didn't like it one bit. I felt alone when a business relationship proved to not be the best place for me. I had thought I was set for life. I had trusted my business associates, but things changed. The current stopped flowing downstream for me. However, it was during this unexpected and unplanned event in my life, in the mid-1980s, that my love of writing was accelerated and the human capital development company that has taken me around the world was set in motion. While in the midst of my upstream swim—walking away from a career choice that initially had brought me great acclaim and recognition—I had to refocus and restart my inward search for the next phase of my life. I too had to pivot and turn in a different direction. Outside positive counsel is great, but being able to pull counsel from your own experience is even better. I would keep telling myself, "I have a problem, but I am not picking cotton off Highway 436. I am in the Red Top Cab."

Looking back at that challenging time in my life, I realize that this was when I began to understand the power and impact of the shift in thinking I had made earlier in my life. At this time I also remembered my porch people and their will to live beyond the rigors of their legally segregated world. I now knew that, for them, swimming upstream was a daily task. I had seen them make those strokes. Although the change in my career was unexpected, I knew that the next move was mine. Recalling the wins from back home—wins that were surrounded by legal segregation, I came to the conclusion that in the midst of well-laid plans, stuff happens, but new pathways can also be discovered.

Clifton L. Taulbert

Don't be surprised when very few people want to join you when you are swimming upstream. In fact, you will be so focused on getting your stuff together that interactions with others will be at a minimum. When swimming upstream—finding that new niche, working night and day to get your business off dead center, watching all your pennies and pinching them ever so tightly, and giving up your weekends to learn more and play less—you get to test your own sense of character.

It's hard and cumbersome for humans to turn upstream when downstream seems so promising. As I went through this process of self-discovery while swimming upstream, I realized that I had not failed. While the project that I had been involved with had moved, my gifts and talents were still intact. The same skills that had brought me to the project still resided within me—skills that could be applied successfully elsewhere. When I realized that my future was still unfolding, it became another important turning point. We all have our turning point. It might be adding a new product to the line. It might be getting rid of the person you hired and liked but found unsuited to the vision that is driving you. It might be having to take a night class or two to keep on the cutting edge of your industry. It might mean cutting the vacation short in order to install a new system. It might just mean changing your lifestyle to pour more money into the business. It might mean putting in the time to be the best student you can be. The good news, though, is that swimming upstream, even if brought on sometimes by gut-wrenching realities or an opportunity for which you are not prepared, at the end of the day can lead you to that place where you will discover a greater sense of accomplishment. You will emerge having learned principles that will serve you well as you maneuver through your life and within this very dynamic and global marketplace.

This is the reality of the marketplace. First plans don't always work. Life does not always go according to your expectations.

Shift Your Thinking: Win where you stand

This is about entrepreneurial thinking at every level of responsibility—being prepared for the unexpected and the unplanned. Know that your plans, expectations, and assignments can literally change overnight. Such events require these things: being flexible and nimble. When the unexpected happens to entrepreneurs, they may reel for a minute, but then they begin to think of ways to turn the challenge into opportunity. This is what we admire about them. This is also what we can admire about you. Handling this challenge, now turned into opportunity, seems to be built into the character of successful entrepreneurs. However, their winning response to these situations is no secret.

Just for the record, keep in mind that entrepreneurs are human. They are just like us. When smacked in the face with unplanned challenges, they reel. They may even stumble. They have dark days as well. They even think of giving up—but they tend to think that way while getting up.

We thought they were down. We saw them on the ground. The news media had just about counted them out. But they were saying, "I can do this. I will do this." Yes, we celebrate their tenacity and perseverance, their flexibility and passion, all of which becomes part of the thinking process that defines the actions we admire. Entrepreneurial thinking is yours to have. This is what I want for you. You may not be looking at a cab making its way down Highway 436, but you will have your moment, so seize it. Shift your thinking. Win where you stand. It will prepare you for those times when swimming upstream is your only option.

It always seems impossible until it's done.
—Nelson Mandela, antiapartheid revolutionary
and former president of South Africa

Personal Questions to Ponder

Let's take a moment to reflect on where you feel you stand professionally and personally at this very moment.

1. Would you follow your dream if everything and everyone around you were telling you to retreat?
2. Have you had your moment of wanting to quit? What drove you to stay steady?
3. How can you use lessons from impending failure to guide your future?
4. How can the life of Nelson Mandela give you reason to believe that the impossible is possible?

Chapter 7

Resolve to Succeed

Resolve to succeed is the seventh strategy within entrepreneurial thinking. Resolve to succeed first manifested itself in my life when I decided and held fast to my decision that I could be in the backseat of the Red Top Cab. That decision was a decisive moment in my life. And it has followed me throughout my journey. No matter the challenge or the opportunity, I know that I can succeed, I won that battle years ago while standing on that cotton row off Highway 436. From that point going forward, I was determined to not let field work and all it entailed define my existence. This was my personal resolve. Though I had received motivation from the porch people that surrounded me, the resolve to succeed had to come from the inside of me.

I wasn't sure of how my journey from the Mississippi Delta would look, at the time, I had never been out of the state of Mississippi. But I was prepared to travel. This strategy is so important to me. For me, it's a family legacy to pass along. This is what I share with my adult son as he is navigating through the waters of Hollywood—a very competitive career environment. I tell Marshall that it's so important to create a picture of his success in his head and to look at it daily—to win when he is not at his desired destination. I have learned that in the real world, unless we are fortunate, very few people go to bed with our success on their minds. Our success is our job, 24/7.

While in Saint Louis, upon leaving the delta, my first real job was horrible. It was demeaning and reminiscent of being back home in the fields. I was a high school graduate, number one in my class, but I found myself washing dishes. I was hurt and embarrassed, but I had the resolve from Highway 436—the shift in my thinking to keep me focused. I needed that focus. I was in Saint Louis, away from the cotton fields, but not at my destination. I knew that! It was talking with myself at midnight and winning those conversations that got me through that awful time. I just kept counting my small wins. Had I given in to that reality, I feel certain that I would not be where I stand today. I know that a personal resolve to succeed is indeed a powerful strategy. It's a timeless and universal strategy. It will work for you. Entrepreneurs swear by it. But it's not their secret. This resolve to succeed is indeed universal and shows up in lives all over the world, not just in the life of a boy from the Mississippi Delta.

When I think of resolve to succeed, I know this strategy has life beyond the Mississippi Delta. As I inventoried conversations I had heard over the years, and people I had met who had embraced such thinking, I immediately thought of my friendship with Andrew Sudar. Andrew and I were as different as any two guys could be. However, our ways of thinking and looking at life became the bond. Our friendship developed many years ago on a cold winter's day in a Michigan airport. It is a friendship that is still maintained. The airport was cold and empty in the early morning except for the two us: me, the mature black man, and him, the young white man, a senior consultant with Systems Modeling out of Sewickley, Pennsylvania. I later learned that he was a successful business road warrior whose mind-set led him to actively tackle the hard issues of self

Shift Your Thinking: Win where you stand

and determining his own stance. Over the years, I witnessed Andrew's commitment to his personal success, workplace success and the delight he took in doing a stellar job in his consulting work across the country. Listening to him talk about his customers and the plans he put in place would make you think he was the founder of the company where he was employed. He truly embraced an ownership perspective and was quite proud of it.

In my attempt to make sure that this last chapter in my book would strike on all cylinders, I decided to call Andrew in Pittsburgh and talk about how important I felt personal resolve to be to one's ultimate success. I wanted this conversation because I had learned over the years that I could trust Andrew to be honest and forthright in his assessment. He knew of my background and had heard the stories of how I had come to early decisions that still positively impact my life today. I wanted to take him on that cab ride one more time, and to hear of his stories.

He agreed immediately to carve out some time for us to talk. It was about a week later for the call and I could hardly wait to talk with Andrew about how I felt personal resolve to succeed to be a strategy within entrepreneurial thinking. I felt certain that the conversation would resonate with him. The week passed, and finally our time to talk. As we talked, I asked him about the pathway that led to his success as a business consultant. I wasn't sure how he would respond. However Andrew's conversation turned out to be as I suspected. He said that much of his success had to do with his commitment to excellence for himself. He held himself accountable. We talked about a few specific business instances where he had been challenged and won, but it was his immediate response to my idea of "midnight wrestling" that really caught his attention. I had explained that over the years of my life, I had come to welcome those midnight wrestling matches—just me, and those unseen voices headed to the mat. Those were the times I could shout my feelings out loud and own fears that I couldn't bring myself to share with others. Andrew jumped right in and told me about similar conversations with himself: the times he argued his case before the mirror and reread his notes while listening to himself, going over his failures and giving himself high fives over his successes. Andrew is very animated and as we talked by phone, I could imagine him standing in the middle of his room with his cell phone to his ear while walking back and forth and pointing as he talked. According to Andrew, it was during those times, at midnight, that he understood and fully embraced his strengths. He became his own voice of reason. His competition was not so formidable. He knew he could meet his competition head-on. He knew the value of talking to himself—conversations that solidified his resolve to succeed. He reaffirmed his faith in himself and what he had to bring to the table. Such nighttime and private conversations brought about the settling needed to step out with the assurance of a winner. He kept asking, "Clifton, you are getting this aren't you?" But never giving me time to respond. Andrew was in his zone. I was just listening.

We were on the same page. We gave hi-fives through the phone. Though we from different worlds, we had subscribed to the same type of thinking. We were both entrepreneurial thinkers. Andrew's conversation was my conversation. That day in Miss Jeffries's field, I held my conversation with myself. I told myself that one day I would be in the cab, not just admiring those who were. I connected with Andrew's conversation about talking to himself. At the end of those many personal midnight conversations, just as I would, Andrew would come to his own decision, to his personal resolve to succeed—to make the pitch and close the deal. We both concluded that personal

Shift Your Thinking: Win where you stand

resolve to succeed is indeed a driving force in the lives of those we call entrepreneurs, but that it can be exploited by any of us, no matter who we are or where we live on the planet.

We also concluded that such thinking is not held captive by those recognized and celebrated as entrepreneurs. It is available to all of us who are determined to win on all levels in this dynamic marketplace. It is not automatic, however. Your desire to succeed wherever you are will only set the stage for effort you are willing to expend and the attitude you are willing to embrace. Once I decided that I would ride in the Red Top Cab, my attitude and my efforts became the support team I would need. I know this to be the same for Andrew. We are both determined to succeed within our personal lives and within our professional lives, and to embrace the required attitude needed and to put forth the effort required.

So do you want to win in the twenty-first-century marketplace, where change, technology and competition seem to be calling the shots? Do you want to win in life? Of course you do. We all do. However, to do so will require coming to a personal decision, a personal declaration of your intentions—your personal resolve. This is where those midnight conversations come in—bantering back and forth all the issues that must be considered. You've thought it through. You've honestly looked at the issues from all sides and angles, and by now, you are convinced that your decision is the right one. The internal debate is over. You know what you are going to do. You can't wait to face the sunlight. Coming to this decision has not been automatic. It was not a piece of cake as it were. It is the outgrowth of a maturing journey that includes internal conversation with yourself—midnight wrestling, as I call it.

At night, the sounds of the day are quiet. However, your concerns are wide-awake, and at midnight they have your full attention. Let's take a look at how this wrestling match might play out. The ring and the mat are before you. You are emotionally positioned. Your opponents are talking trash—trying to convince you that you don't have what it takes to win. You can't see them, but you can hear them. Fear and insufficient knowledge are trying to pin you down. Half-truths are swirling around your head. They are getting louder and more forceful. You are about ready to question your ability. Old losses are trying to take center stage. You want to get away, the negative voices keep coming, you want to turn your back and leave the ring, but your own voice refuses to let you jump from the ring of decision. The voice of your vision keeps you in the ring. As your vision stands tall in your head, it is in such moments that you begin to realize your strength and your strategies, and in doing so give rise to your resolve to succeed. A settling comes over you. You are ready to take them on. Courage is all over your face. And those negative voices pull back, farther and farther from you. You are back in control of your destiny.

In those midnight wrestling bouts, you will be confronted and comforted by countless voices of others. Some will praise you and cheer you on, but many will attempt to tear you down and question your skills and abilities. Some of those voices will bring up failures you've long since tried to put behind you. The failures will be named and the shame will show up once again, seeking to further tear you down and sway your decision to succeed. You are in effect wrestling with yourself. To come out as a winner with your hands and head held high will ultimately set you apart in the marketplace.

This is what Andrew alluded to and what I fully understand. He faced his opponents, and they had to hear him out. Don't be afraid to be heard out. There can be no better feeling than hearing yourself hold that winning conversation—the last word of your resolve to win. You can win right where you stand!

Shift Your Thinking: Win where you stand

We have all had those mental midnight wrestling matches and will continue to do so. This comes with life. It comes with our decision to be a player in the marketplace.

To leave that ring after three rounds convinced of your ability to win is to set your resolve in stone. A resolve set in stone is what you need to maintain your position and to succeed in today's marketplace.

When they are alone in the world and no one is handing out accolades and invitations to openings, entrepreneurs often find themselves wrestling with plans and the many conversations they have had with others. But don't rue such nights. Just know that you can come out with a decisive win. This happens to Silicon Valley entrepreneurs as often as it does to those who may have just started their ventures. These feelings and subsequent midnight conversations happens across the spectrum of us—from innovators, educators, students, employees to corporate CEOs. And when they show up in your head, nervousness sets in as you contemplate your next move on the mat.

That's when you, as the entrepreneurial thinker, should rely on your vision and dare this new, emotionally draining reality to diminish your drive to win. You know you are in a match, but you also have the mind-set of one who can win. You can't win or lose if you aren't in the ring.

When these challenging moments show up, those with this entrepreneurial way of thinking ready themselves for the wrestling match. Just as Andrew said, they accept the fact that they are going to have to talk to themselves. Being in the ring brings out multiple voices, all vying for your attention. It can be confusing. It's easy to think about walking away. However, entrepreneurial thinkers refuse to just walk away. Instead, while in the ring, they look for that winning "hold" that's going to deliver the moment of resolve they need. The winners are those who move through these midnight rounds and come out with their own resolution to succeed. They face the truth, discard the lies, and discover their gifts of strength, analytical skill, courage, and fortitude. They are now prepared for that winning conversation.

Speaking of "a winning conversation," consider the sixteenth president of the United States, Abraham Lincoln. From my perspective, his winning the presidency had much to do with his ability to come to his own conclusive resolution to win. In counseling with a friend earlier in his career, Lincoln had admonished the friend to trust and value his personal resolution to succeed, saying that this was more important than any other thing. This should be the same conclusion that you personally come to after listening to all those midnight voices in your head.

Somewhere in the midst of listening to and pinning down those negative voices, you too will be able to draw strength from every failure, and courage from every win, no matter how small. This becomes personal discovery time. You will discover that your failures were real but not paralyzing, and you will now be energized to look at what you had once considered small wins and discover a positive trend that is uniquely yours—a trend that can be useful to winning big in the marketplace.

Just know that your personal resolve is powerful and can move mountains. It's absolutely essential to get you in the game with the right attitude—an attitude that can become positively contagious. This becomes the attitude you want to see trickle down to others who might be looking up to you. Once in the marketplace, this same resolve can take you even farther. Inside your head, you can hear your own voice saying, "I can do this. I will do this." When you hear those eight positive words ringing clearly in your head, I want you to let them ring loudly from your lips, too. Hear yourself saying that the game isn't over and that you have just begun. You can be a

Shift Your Thinking: Win where you stand

competitor. You can be a real player in the marketplace. You can ensure that your business has a lasting shelf life, whether it provides a product or a service. In your business, you want both your efforts and those of your team to promote positive conversations after your service has been rendered and your product delivered. Your resolve to win translates into commitment and accountability in action, both of which your support team will need if your business is to ensure that positive, after-the-delivery conversation.

When the lives of entrepreneurs are closely examined, the results of their personal commitment and accountability—driven by their sense of ownership and personal resolve—begin to emerge. I have found this to be true in my own life. You just don't ever give up. Your business will need this level of commitment if it is to win in today's highly competitive, challenging, and changing environment. Your commitment to manage the changes and challenges you face also emerges upon winning those midnight wrestling matches.

Now that you have won a match or two and have come to your own resolution to succeed, you are positioned to move forward with the confidence necessary to drive your personal actions or to engage your team. If you are leading a team, such actions clearly demonstrate to them that they are with a winner and that together you will win even more. This becomes the conversation that is taken home or shared on the golf course, during a pick-up basketball game, in the local pub, or around the television while watching the game with a friend—or, in my case, watching the Oklahoma City Thunder's Kevin Durant work his magic one more time.

A winning resolve doesn't just show up. It's the result of much internal wrestling—taking into account all of one's experiences, both those that were good and those that were disappointing.

As you move through life, storing up personal experiences is inevitable, and how you choose to face and utilize those experiences will determine your entrepreneurial outcome. Your personal resolve becomes your secret weapon to win. When in the face of daunting challenges, your vision remains intact. When the naysayers, the pundits, and even close business associates, or family and friends call for surrender, you stand firm.

Stand firm!

Before I close this chapter on the power of personal resolve, let's go back to 1860 and the nomination of Abraham Lincoln as the Republican candidate for president of the United States. Keep in mind that he was not expected to win. He was an unlikely candidate. Maybe, when looked at from the outside, his detractors were right. His past was filled with failures, which his opponents sought to capitalize on. Many in the eastern political establishment—states like New York, New Jersey, and Pennsylvania—wanted him to back out. He chose not to do so. Let me repeat this: he chose not to do so. He heard his own voice. You can hear your own voice too.

How did Abraham Lincoln come to such a decision with so many naysayers at his heels? I can only imagine that he had his midnight wrestling matches—dealing with the voices of others trying to shape his political decision. When the family was asleep and he stood alone, I can imagine the voices of dissent became loud and clear in his head. Yet he couldn't just walk away. The win was the presidency. Conversation was demanded. He had to bring his own unique moves to the ring of contemplation. I can imagine him reliving his failed attempts and almost agreeing with those who sought to keep him out of the race. His failures were real.

I can see Lincoln's thoughts traveling back in time to when he was a young lawyer, losing some cases but continuing on, running for various offices and mostly losing, but

Shift Your Thinking: Win where you stand

continuing on. While enveloped in his midnight wrestling match with multiple voices, he could not help but relive all the comments being made by the eastern branch of his party. They questioned his ability and reminded others of what they perceived to be his backwardness and his seeming lack of command of the king's language. Yet he held firm. He was determined to get his hold on the matter at hand. Holding firm has everything to do with your will to win, whatever your goal might be.

As for President Lincoln, I can also imagine him finally sitting down in his well-worn rocking chair, looking out at the darkness of the night, and recalling his victories—naming them one by one. No matter how small or inconsequential these victories may have seemed to the opposing members from his Republican Party, they were of significance to him. As his mind crystallized around those victories, he realized that his efforts mattered. Your efforts matter—thus the need to put them forth. Slowly but surely, Lincoln began to see his strengths, his ability to keep getting up when verbally pinned down by others. His seemingly small steps of success were now becoming great strides in his thinking, and the voices of the naysayers were losing their hold over his mind. Instead they were being pinned down with such a force of will that they couldn't escape. He had won right where he stood! He had shifted his own thinking and moved away from the noise and clutter of others.

Now experiencing this sense of issues being settled, I can imagine his tall and lanky body now slowly getting up from his rocking chair and rising to its full height. I can picture him looking out on the darkness of the night and the stars that hold their own. Now with a knowing smile on his face, one that his whole person can feel, he walks out of the small room he uses as his study to the bedroom where his wife, Mary Todd Lincoln, is asleep. She wakes up when he comes in and asks if all is well.

He smiles and reassures her that all is well. He reaches over and pulls the sheet closer around the collar of her nightgown, leans down, and brushes a kiss across her lips as he says, "You are going to make a great First Lady."

Lincoln had come to the resolution he needed, a personal resolution that he would transfer to his team—a way of thinking and approaching his campaign, and with which he would eventually capture the attention of the nation. I dare not think of the state of our country had we missed out on his incredible leadership. We almost did. Never underestimate what you have to offer. Wrestle to win.

Without question, there is a definite place for personal resolve in the twenty-first-century marketplace. The uncertainty of this marketplace and growing competitive forces bring moments of angst and anxiety, but it can also bring opportunity. I know that if entrepreneurial thinking is embraced, personal resolve will show up, not as a gift without effort but as the outcome of emotional struggle—wrestling at midnight.

The challenges you may be facing today through circumstances both beyond your control and perhaps of your own making call for the type of personal leadership that refuses to allow you to abdicate the vision that started your journey. Stay in your Red Top Cab!

This resolve is not something you can touch or feel, or cut a piece of and share with others, but it is contagious nonetheless, and in a sense it is transferrable. It's that internal emotional and positive resolution that bolsters your confidence in such a way that others are led to join with you because they have watched how you respond to the challenges and opportunities you face.

You see this all the time when the media celebrates a successful entrepreneurial endeavor. There is always that moment where praise is given to those who, in the face of adversity, stood by their resolve to succeed. The barriers the entrepreneurs

Shift Your Thinking: Win where you stand

faced were real. They could have pulled the plug midstream and walked away. But they didn't quit. They stayed with it until they won. Their committed support team did likewise. Displaying such a resolve has positive impact upon others. This is the linchpin to victory. This is what we really celebrate.

I have little doubt that for those entrepreneurs we celebrate as winners, their victory was due to the internal personal resolve to succeed—the ability to come to a firm internal decision, to find a solution to the problems they faced, and to embrace opportunities that others had not seen. This is what social and economic research says about the men and women to whom we ascribe the moniker of "entrepreneur." Today I am telling you that you can win. Your leadership can be stellar, your business can be a success, and your plan can be realized. Your career can be amazing. This strategy is personal but powerful. I want you to be on top of your game and fully aware of the power of your own resolve to succeed. Remember, this strategy is not a secret, but it's your secret weapon. Employing your personal resolve to win is within your power.

The nation was a beneficiary of President Lincoln's personal resolve. I was a beneficiary of the resolve of my porch people. In the 1950s Mississippi Delta, those same porch people, my early influencers, certainly had roadblocks and barriers in their way, but they kept their resolve despite the daily grind of cotton work. Legal segregation was a way of life—an officially sanctioned way of life. At that time, there was little they could do to change the status quo. They had to deal with the deck of cards given them. This is what still amazes me today: their personal resolve was not altered. They possessed that internal ability to firmly decide to face their challenges head-on, and then in their own way to win where they stood. They first won where important: in their heads and in the fields where they worked. You may find this difficult to believe, but while working in a field they didn't own, they were looking to the future. I watched as they raised small sums of money to send off to their kin in college and also insisted that funds be set aside monthly to take care of burial expenses. In their unselfishness, the lengthening steps of their children became the vision they embraced. They were looking to a future. They taught me to do the same. I want to pass this universal and timeless strategy along to you.

For whoever you are—employer, entrepreneur, independent sales associate, educator, student, or employee—and wherever you are on your journey to success, perhaps this quote from President Lincoln will shed a bit more light on how important the process of coming to your personal resolution to succeed truly is: "If you are resolutely determined...the thing is more than half done already."

Somewhere along the way, long before Appomattox, I feel that Lincoln won the Civil War in his heart. Saving the nation was his focus. His earlier wrestling and his decision to stand firm would continue to influence his actions and those who would become part of his administration. He knew the value of embracing a personal resolution to succeed. He embraced the gumption that defined him. He operated from such a resolve that would eventually save the nation, end the war, and start the unraveling of the stranglehold of slavery—so important to me and to our nation.

This seventh strategy, Resolve to Succeed is another key to your success. It will hold everything together and validates your choice of mind-set. If Lincoln had embraced a fixed mind-set, he would never have won the presidency. Had he not been prepared for hard work, he would never have been able to assemble his team. In matters of importance, he knew what was going on and demanded the same of his team. He was attuned to the health metrics of a nation.

No matter where you find yourself today, and no matter what your profession, remember that people are at the

Shift Your Thinking: Win where you stand

center. How these relationships are handled internally and externally will speak to the success of your ventures wherever they are and whatever they might be. Your personal resolve matters. It can win a presidency, keep a nation together, and start unraveling the institution of slavery. It can also marshal the imagination of African American entrepreneurs at the turn of the twentieth century in such a way that they would leave their homes in other states to find their dreams in what was known as the Indian and Oklahoma Territories. These were African American families—pioneers, if you will. They knew the sting of legal segregation, and there were those among them that had experienced the sting of slavery itself. However, they were determined to succeed. Without the teaching of Dr. Carol Dweck of Stanford University to guide them, they had intuitively gravitated toward the growth mind-set. They were determined. They had built a solid relationship bridge among themselves and those who reach across the barriers. Because of their entrepreneurial way of thinking, they played the hand dealt them beyond expectations.

Over time these African American men and women who were resolved to succeed built their dream—a place called Deep Greenwood. This prosperous African American conclave of businesses in the late 1890s and early 1920s became known as the Negro Wall Street of America (a.k.a. Black Wall Street). J. B. Stradford, a son of a freed Kentucky slave, built on Greenwood his field of dreams, the Stradford Hotel, with all the modern conveniences of his day. There were also the Williams's buildings and their Dreamland Theater—built and owned by this African American couple—that would seat 750 paying customers. Driven by their growth mind-set, these entrepreneurs were determined to do the heavy lifting required to turn their dreams into their reality. They were not called "entrepreneurs," but they had tapped into that way of ughout your life and will impact your response to the six remaining straI knew from the delta and a term that was familiar to them, they dared legal segregation to hold them back or the sting of slavery experienced to kill their dream. Though their world would come to a tragic end in 1921, it was not before they were able to see their dreams fulfilled before their eyes. For them, the impossible had indeed become possible. Resolving to succeed is indeed a life-changing strategy and continues to be so all over the world.

Our personal resolve tells us that we can win and that we have the stuff of winners. It tells us that we can walk on the moon.

With this knowledge, it's time to flex your muscles of personal leadership and performance. Although easy is not guaranteed, with your own personal resolve, you can win. Resolve to succeed wherever you stand—just starting out, in your cubicle, in the corner office, teaching a class, attending a class, starting a business, growing a business, or employed by a business.

Keep in mind that you will have challenges. Every age has them. I had mine, and I still have them. You will have yours. However, challenges are the threads woven through victory, and every age has also left clear examples of those who won. We have their stories in biographies. We have their lives in film. We have conversation from those who saw their ascents firsthand. We must do the same: leave our footprints showing where we traveled on our way to succeeding. Why not make the next winner *you*? Someone you may never meet might just benefit from your story, from your shift in thinking and your resolve to win where you stood. It's your move.

Always bear in mind that your own *resolution to* succeed *is more important than any one thing.*
—Abraham Lincoln,
sixteenth president of the United States of America

Shift Your Thinking: Win where you stand

Personal Questions to Ponder

Let's take a moment to reflect on where you feel you stand professionally and personally at this very moment.

1. When did you first experience a midnight wrestling match? Who won?
2. What was your most recent match like? How did it turn out?
3. How do you plan to introduce the importance of personal resolve to your team?
4. What will you take away from the lessons of President Lincoln?

In Conclusion

It is so easy to do what we have always done. It's easy to see the success of others and not envision our own. This is the fixed mind-set. Such a mind-set does not lead you down a path to success. For the most part, it is comfortable with things as they are, thus potentially sabotaging your future. Your mind-set will always be key to your thinking and to the actions you employ. Choose the growth mind-set and transform your life. Choose the growth mind-set and become your own example of an entrepreneurial thinker. Be willing to go beyond the expected and to set aside the average and the comfortable. You deserve more. This is what we celebrate in those who employ entrepreneurial thinking as a way of living their lives. Hopefully this book has challenged your thinking and motivated you to be in charge of your destiny—to employ these seven strategies so that you too can win right where you stand.

As that young boy in the cotton rows of the delta, I watched for years as others moved in and out of our lives, leaving the fields and a way of life that many felt would last forever. I admired them and the cabs that ferried them to and fro. For the longest time, I didn't see myself emulating them. I wish that I could remember exactly what happened that caused my change of mind. Maybe I heard others talking about going beyond where they were, and somehow I was captivated by these people who had found ways to live beyond the culture that surrounded us and the fields that sought to define us. It could have been their positive talk in an environment so opposite that finally caused me to realize that I could dream as well.

And one day I did. When that Red Top Cab came rolling down that blacktop highway, I was no longer focused on someone else. My thinking had shifted. I saw me in the backseat. I became the subject of my internal conversations. I was still in the fields, but I had won. I had won where I stood. This is what I want for you: to know that you can win right where you stand. Where you are is your starting place.

Change did not come overnight, or even in weeks or months, but I knew that I was different. Something had ignited on the inside and would eventually be visible to others. Maybe it was the story Mama Ponk always told about visiting her son Melvin in Detroit that seeded my thinking. We need to know the journeys of others as we prepare our own. Their journeys become the maps we read to get to the destination we desire. In this book, *Shift Your Thinking: Win Where You Stand*, I have tried to infuse the stories of others with my own journey to further bolster your will to win and to lead you to not settle for less than your full potential. I want this conversation to have been meaningful and for you to have gleaned nuggets that speak specifically to you, right where you stand. There are those that will enable you to maximize your efforts and embrace a dynamic way of thinking that can positively impact all areas of your life. This is part of entrepreneurial thinking: "I can do this! I will do this!" Such an attitude will serve you well. It will show up wherever you are and in whatever position you currently hold.

Within our respective marketplaces, we can all benefit from this way of thinking and looking at the world that surrounds us. It has meant everything to me. I dread to think what course my life might have taken had I not been exposed to men and women, my influencers, who seemed to have intuitively understood that my thinking mattered in the outcome of my life. This

Shift Your Thinking: Win where you stand

is a truism with consequences far beyond the world in which I grew up. Their belief in embracing the ability within you to change your circumstances and grow productively is timeless and universal. This is what we celebrate in those we define as entrepreneurs. Such thinking refuses to let you give up. You just keep moving forward.

In 2008, great economic minds gathered from around the world in Switzerland to engage in the World Economic Forum, where they produced important documents for nations to review as they made plans and economic predictions for our future. A very meaningful statement was embedded within the document they produced: *"Everyone can benefit from an entrepreneurial experience."*

In those seven words, they took the mystique out of entrepreneurship. They recognized that embedded within the efforts and outcomes of those called entrepreneurs was a way of thinking and looking at the world that could be of great benefit to each of us as we set out to lead our lives and maximize our potential. This includes you. Whether you are starting or running a business, an employee in a business, or a student at a significant crossroad, you have to ask yourself several key questions:

1) **Am I willing to shift my thinking?**
2) **Am I willing to do the hard work required?**
3) **Do I value an inclusive and collaborative culture?**
4) **Am I willing to be intentional about bringing others along?**
5) **Will I tend to the details?**
6) **Will I accept challenges head-on?**
7) **Will I stand my ground?**

These are very legitimate questions to be asked by all, regardless of our professional or personal setting. After all, the responses will say volumes about the mind-set you have embraced and the subsequent actions taken. These are questions I continually ask myself. And I feel that my early influencers had a sense of these seven questions and in their own ways set out to answer them though they represent a different place and time. Whatever the time period and however the goals might be defined, these seven inside entrepreneurial thinking strategies will aid you in the shift of your thinking and in maintaining the momentum needed for your success. No matter where you live or what kind of work you do, the conclusion is that embracing an entrepreneurial way of thinking can take your efforts to another level—a level of success that can set you apart as a winner.

Embrace the opportunity to choose the growth mind-set as you set out to make your mark in life and in industry. Don't settle. We can all live beyond limitations that seem to be forever. ***Our commitment to diligence, hard work, and education can expand our opportunities.***

When we embrace Dr. Dweck's growth mind-set, we also place importance on being determined. To be determined is to accept as normal the heavy lifting required to be successful. Entrepreneurs know and embrace this reality. You can do likewise. You are not looking for shortcuts, just the right and sustainable ways to win. In so doing, your hard work becomes your ally, and you will find yourself creating new and exciting pathways. Keep in mind too that people matter and that you must commit to building a solid relationship bridge. Building solid relationships will serve your vision to succeed well.

People matter. Mentors matter. Your team matters. You matter. The process of building this bridge creates the sustainable culture you will need to keep yourself and your team focused and engaged. This bridge is needed, but it doesn't show up automatically. The people that support your efforts,

Shift Your Thinking: Win where you stand

both internal and external team members, all need to see RAI—respect, affirmation, and inclusion—in action throughout your organization. These qualities are key to relationship building. Slow down to lead so that you can be reflective and thoughtful in the signals you send. You want to ensure that you bring others along through productive followership. These should be people not just hired and on the payroll, but vision focused and mission driven. Remember, your people will do what they see you do. Many entrepreneurs are known for leading by involvement: Steve Jobs, Oprah Winfrey, Sam Walton, Tyler Perry and the list continues. Oftentimes this internal involvement spills over into the communities where they live. If you want your team to rally to the cause, then as a leader you must give them reason to do so. Leadership signals matter! I would say the several entrepreneurs listed have given their team members reason to embrace the mission and vision. No one listed would have been able to make their vision come true if not for the team alongside of them.

Know your business health metrics. In your business, be fully aware of what you have to watch and measure and the importance of the whole team being involved in the watching and measuring process. Know your life metrics as well. Talk about those expectations, and when they are being met, celebrate. However, if they are not being met, you can't afford to simply hope and wish, just as in a staff meeting, you must be prepared to recalibrate your agenda to make sure that the plan is following the vision and the mission. In life and in work, it's important to keep your eyes on the ball. Keep your eyes on the ball is not just for those defined as leaders, but for the entire team.

I know many of you are excited about this world of business and all the real and rumored perks that come along in this dynamic marketplace. But remember, owning your own business is a journey—one where success will ultimately be defined by the consistency of the efforts you expend. It doesn't matter what the glossy prints display or how many stories they write about successful entrepreneur moguls: easy is not guaranteed. **It wasn't guaranteed for them, and it will not be guaranteed for you.** Be prepared for those days when the unplanned and unexpected show up and a completely new strategy is required. Be prepared to swim upstream. You have the ability to do so. You will exercise new creative muscles and sharpen your focus, and in so doing you will make lasting and important discoveries. That anxious moment can become the creative fuel that drives you beyond the ordinary.

Lastly, you are more likely to win in the marketplace if you personally resolve to succeed. Teams win when each member becomes a winner—hence the need to recognize the importance of your internal decision-making process. Part of this process usually involves those times when you are all alone at midnight, struggling with questions and second-guessing answers. Don't rue those internal midnight wrestling matches. For many of us, these are the times where personal resolutions to win are formed. Go all three rounds and come out a winner. Remember, it's up to you. Shifting your thinking is where you start. This will lead you to choosing the right mind-set—a mind-set that can take you down a path beyond your childhood imagination.

While I was growing up in the delta, Australia was simply a small spot on a rather large world map, but not a place that I would see in my lifetime. At that time, I was happy just to get to Greenville, only twenty-eight miles north of me. Life changed. I was unaware at the time, but my Red Top Cab had Australia on my agenda, and some forty-five years later, in this year of 2014, I found myself in this country as the opening speaker for a celebration of small-business entrepreneurs and their connections

Shift Your Thinking: Win where you stand

to much larger industry supply chains. I shared with my new mates my own journey from the fields of the delta to the world of entrepreneurship. When talking to the Aboriginal community in Dubbo, Australia, I could say without question that my life hasn't been without challenges. But I also left them a clear picture of not stopping, but one of taking a deep breath and swimming upstream. I wanted them to know that they could do likewise. They could win where they were standing and take that winning mind-set along with them throughout the rest of their journey. Though I know that easy is not guaranteed, I have come to believe that the impossible is possible. Never allow your circumstances to limit your dreams. Always strive to be what you dream!

You could very well become the next Sara Rotman, Mark Cuban, Chester Cadieux, Steve Jobs, Clay Clark, Reginald Lewis, or Oprah Winfrey, for that matter. More importantly, you can be your best self—successful and fulfilled because you have employed a way of thinking that will allow you to maximize your potential in whatever field you choose. From a once-prosperous African American community called Greenwood's Black Wall Street to a young boy in a cotton field in the Mississippi Delta, to Southwest Airlines' start, to QuikTrip in Tulsa, Oklahoma, to Kevin Durant on the basketball court, to Mark Zuckerberg changing the way we communicate, to Nate Waters having lived a full life beyond the barriers that could have held him back and to you, entrepreneurial thinking has challenged and continue to challenge individuals to succeed where they stand.

The Frenchman Alexis de Tocqueville was right in his nineteenth-century observation, with all of Europe as his backdrop, when he concluded that a "new and powerful" nation can emerge on the scene as a result of a free, original, and inventive mind. Knowing that you can shift your thinking, be creative and

inventive is at the heart of entrepreneurial thinking and winning where you stand. Entrepreneurial thinking, from my perspective, is saying to yourself and those around you, "I can do this, and I will do this." **It's your move!**
Shift your thinking: win where you stand!

About the Author

CLIFTON L. TAULBERT

According to Clifton L. Taulbert, noted author and entrepreneur, he could have failed had he not encountered entrepreneurial thinkers and community builders early on in his life. Taulbert was born on the Mississippi Delta during the era of legal segregation, where opportunities were few and barriers were plentiful. However, Taulbert dreamed of being successful, even when he didn't know the shape that his success would take. While picking cotton in the delta, he dreamed, but he never imagined that he would grow up to become a writer to lecture in the US Capitol Rotunda, or to be asked by former US Supreme Court Justice Sandra Day O'Connor to be a lecturer to many of her peers and their invited guests. Taulbert credits entrepreneurial thinking and his "porch people builders of community" for those invitations.

After successfully serving in the 89th Presidential Wing of the United States Air Force in the 1960s, Taulbert was honorably discharged and started the journey that he continues today—dreaming beyond his circumstances. This is how Taulbert describes the mind of the entrepreneur, a mind-set he believes to be available to any and all of us. With college completed and graduate work in banking under his belt (Oral Roberts University and the Southwest Graduate School of Banking at Southern Methodist University), Taulbert embarked upon one of his childhood dreams—owning his own business. Though his elders in the Mississippi Delta had very little, they wisely shared their dreams and possibilities with Taulbert, and he wisely embraced what he saw and heard.

In 1985, Taulbert formed the Freemount Corporation, a diversified marketing and consulting company, which led to his involvement with the original team that introduced the StairMaster exercise system to the world. Taulbert went on to grow Freemount Consulting into a leadership and human capital development company with an international reach. Taulbert uses his book *Eight Habits of the Heart*—with copies now on every continent—to teach and facilitate with audiences worldwide on how these eight timeless principles can transform lives and communities. Especially notable is his work about building a culture of community in the workplace where our diversity is welcomed. Taulbert challenges his audiences to embrace RAI (Respect, Affirmation and Inclusion) as the principles to embrace and live out.

Taulbert serves as a knowledge source content provider to Korn Ferry, a company that empowers businesses and leaders worldwide to reach their goals. He has contributed to *Leader to Leader*, an international leadership journal formerly published by the Peter Drucker Institute. He has conducted lectures and workshops at the Harvard University Principals Center, the United States Air Force Academy, Darden School of Business, NATO, Lockheed Martin, Bank of America, FDIC, the Department of Justice, and Wrigley's, among others.

In 2011, Taulbert stretched his reach to Rwanda when he became a managing partner in African Bean Company, an

African American-owned, nationally certified coffee brand in the United States, the home of Roots Java coffee brand.

CLIFTON L. TAULBERT: THE WRITER

Taulbert's first book, *Once Upon A Time When We Were Colored*, became an international best seller, a major motion picture, and a gift to Nelson Mandela from the United States. Taulbert's second book, *The Last Train North*, was nominated for the Pulitzer Prize. Taulbert recently introduced his thirteenth book, *The Invitation*, a seven-year project intended to ignite a meaningful conversation on community and race in America—the impact and the promise.

CLIFTON L. TAULBERT INVOLVED

Trustee of the University of Tulsa and board member of the following: the National Character Education Partnership Education Advisory Council; Tulsa Area Salvation Army; Tulsa Historical Society; Natchez Literary and Cinema Celebration; Oklahoma for Excellence—David Boren's organization for recognizing high school students' exceptional talents; the advisory board of the Eudora Welty Foundation; and the board of reference for the Movie Guide Award and Oral Roberts University. He is a founding member of the Anne Kathryn Taulbert Sickle Cell Fund.

HONORS:

Chosen by CNN at the turn of the millennium to be one of the voices of community; inducted into the United States Enlisted Airmen Hall of Fame; honored with the National Jewish Humanitarian of the Year Award and as Arthritis Foundation Volunteer of the Year; received the NAACP's 27th Annual Image Award for contribution to literature; Pulitzer Prize nominee for *The Last Train North*; first African American to win the Mississippi Institute of Arts and Letters Award for Nonfiction; and in 2005, inducted into the SMEI Academy of Achievement: The Free Enterprise System.

FAMILY

Taulbert shares his life with his wife, Barbara, and their adult son, Marshall Danzy Taulbert, an aspiring actor and writer in Los Angeles.